Photoshop® Elements 4
Top 100

Simplified®

TIPS & TRICKS

by Mike and Linda Wooldridge

Visual

WILEY

Photoshop® Elements 4: Top 100 Simplified® Tips & Tricks

Published by
Wiley Publishing, Inc.
111 River Street
Hoboken, NJ 07030-5774

Published simultaneously in Canada

Copyright © 2006 by Wiley Publishing, Inc., Indianapolis, Indiana

Library of Congress Control Number: 2005933667

ISBN-13: 978-0-471-77798-4

ISBN-10: 0-471-77798-6

Manufactured in the United States of America

10 9 8 7 6 5 4 3 2 1

1K/RX/RR/QV/IN

Trademark Acknowledgments

Contact Us

For general information on our other products and services contact our Customer Care Department within the U.S. at 800-762-2974, outside the U.S. at 317-572-3993 or fax 317-572-4002.

For technical support please visit www.wiley.com/techsupport.

WILEY

Wiley Publishing, Inc.

U.S. Sales

Contact Wiley at
(800) 762-2974 or
fax (317) 572-4002.

PRAISE FOR VISUAL BOOKS

"I have to praise you and your company on the fine products you turn out. I have twelve Visual books in my house. They were instrumental in helping me pass a difficult computer course. Thank you for creating books that are easy to follow. Keep turning out those quality books."

Gordon Justin (Brielle, NJ)

"What fantastic teaching books you have produced! Congratulations to you and your staff. You deserve the Nobel prize in Education. Thanks for helping me understand computers."

Bruno Tonon (Melbourne, Australia)

"A Picture Is Worth A Thousand Words! If your learning method is by observing or hands-on training, this is the book for you!"

Lorri Pegan-Durastante (Wickliffe, OH)

"Over time, I have bought a number of your 'Read Less - Learn More' books. For me, they are THE way to learn anything easily. I learn easiest using your method of teaching."

José A. Mazón (Cuba, NY)

"You've got a fan for life!! Thanks so much!!"

Kevin P. Quinn (Oakland, CA)

"I have several books from the Visual series and have always found them to be valuable resources."

Stephen P. Miller (Ballston Spa, NY)

"I have several of your Visual books and they are the best I have ever used."

Stanley Clark (Crawfordville, FL)

"Like a lot of other people, I understand things best when I see them visually. Your books really make learning easy and life more fun."

John T. Frey (Cadillac, MI)

"I have quite a few of your Visual books and have been very pleased with all of them. I love the way the lessons are presented!"

Mary Jane Newman (Yorba Linda, CA)

"Thank you, thank you, thank you...for making it so easy for me to break into this high-tech world."

Gay O'Donnell (Calgary, Alberta,Canada)

"I write to extend my thanks and appreciation for your books. They are clear, easy to follow, and straight to the point. Keep up the good work! I bought several of your books and they are just right! No regrets! I will always buy your books because they are the best."

Seward Kollie (Dakar, Senegal)

"I would like to take this time to thank you and your company for producing great and easy-to-learn products. I bought two of your books from a local bookstore, and it was the best investment I've ever made! Thank you for thinking of us ordinary people."

Jeff Eastman (West Des Moines, IA)

"Compliments to the chef!! Your books are extraordinary! Or, simply put, extra-ordinary, meaning way above the rest! THANKYOU THANKYOU THANKYOU! I buy them for friends, family, and colleagues."

Christine J. Manfrin (Castle Rock, CO)

CREDITS

Project Editor
Robyn Siesky

Acquisitions Editor
Jody Lefevere

Product Development Manager
Lindsay Sandman

Copy Editor
Marylouise Wiack

Technical Editor
Dennis Short

Editorial Manager
Robyn Siesky

Permissions Editor
Laura Moss

Editorial Assistant
Adrienne Porter

Manufacturing
Allan Conley
Linda Cook
Paul Gilchrist
Jennifer Guynn

Indexer
Lynnzee Elze

Book Design
Kathie Rickard

Production Coordinator
Maridee Ennis

Layout
Carrie Foster
Denny Hager
Jennifer Heleine
Amanda Spagnuolo

Screen Artist
Jill A. Proll

Illustrator
Ronda David-Burroughs

Cover Design
Anthony Bunyan

Proofreader
Tricia Liebig

Quality Control
Laura Albert
Susan Moritz

Vice President and Executive Group Publisher
Richard Swadley

Vice President and Publisher
Barry Pruett

Composition Director
Debbie Stailey**

ABOUT THE AUTHORS

Mike Wooldridge is a technology writer and Web developer in the San Francisco Bay Area. He has written more than a dozen books in the Visual series. **Linda Wooldridge** is a former senior editor at Macworld and author of *Teach Yourself Visually Adobe Photoshop CS2*. For access to some of the example images used in this book, visit: www.mediacosm.com/elements.

HOW TO USE THIS BOOK

Photoshop® Elements 4: Top 100 Simplified® Tips & Tricks includes 100 tasks that reveal cool secrets, teach timesaving tricks, and explain great tips guaranteed to make you more productive with Photoshop Elements 4. The easy-to-use layout lets you work through all the tasks from beginning to end or jump in at random.

Who Is This Book For?

You already know Photoshop Elements 4 basics. Now you'd like to go beyond, with shortcuts, tricks, and tips that let you work smarter and faster. And because you learn more easily when someone *shows* you how, this is the book for you.

Conventions Used in This Book

❶ Steps

This book uses step-by-step instructions to guide you easily through each task. Numbered callouts on every screen shot show you exactly how to perform each task, step by step.

❷ Tips

Practical tips provide insights to save you time and trouble, caution you about hazards to avoid, and reveal how to do things in Photoshop Elements 4 that you never thought possible!

❸ Task Numbers

Task numbers from 1 to 100 indicate which lesson you are working on.

❹ Difficulty Levels

For quick reference, the symbols below mark the difficulty level of each task.

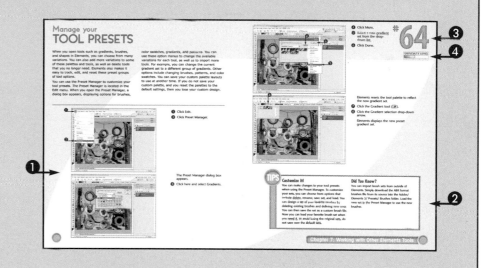

DIFFICULTY LEVEL	Demonstrates a new spin on a common task
DIFFICULTY LEVEL	Introduces a new skill or a new task
DIFFICULTY LEVEL	Combines multiple skills requiring in-depth knowledge
DIFFICULTY LEVEL	Requires extensive skill and may involve other technologies

Table of Contents

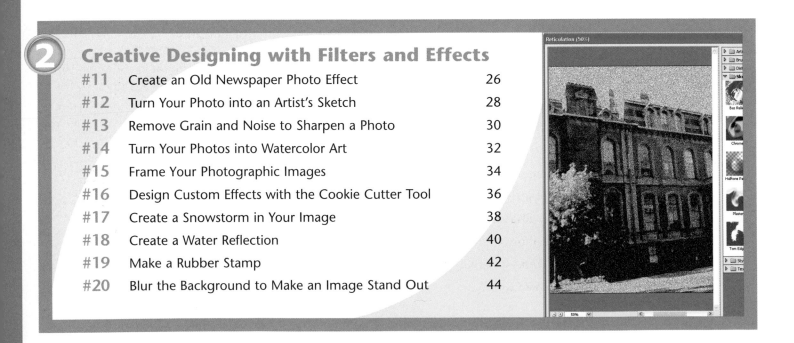

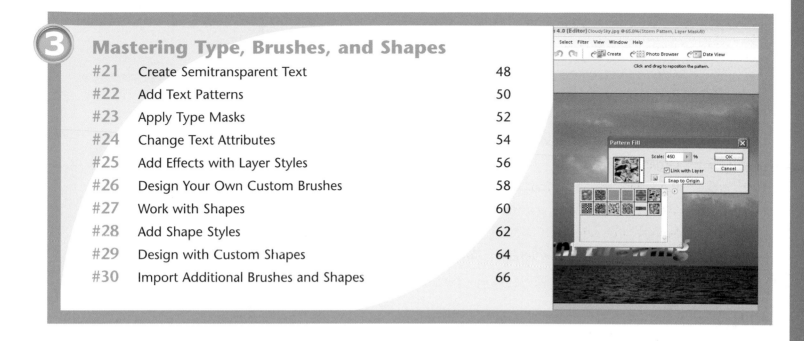

Mastering Type, Brushes, and Shapes

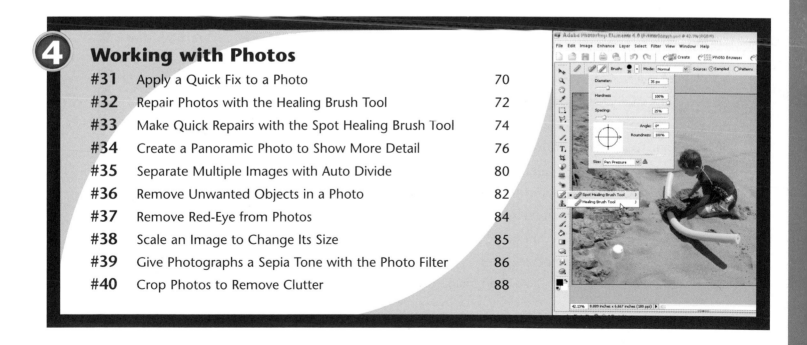

Working with Photos

Table of Contents

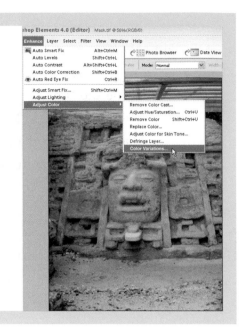

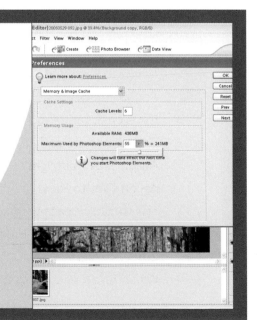

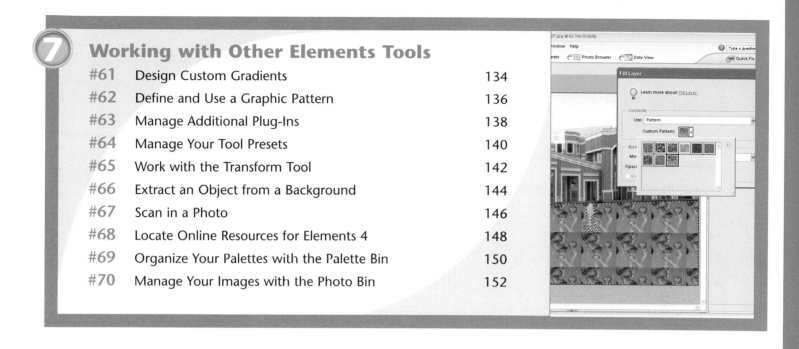

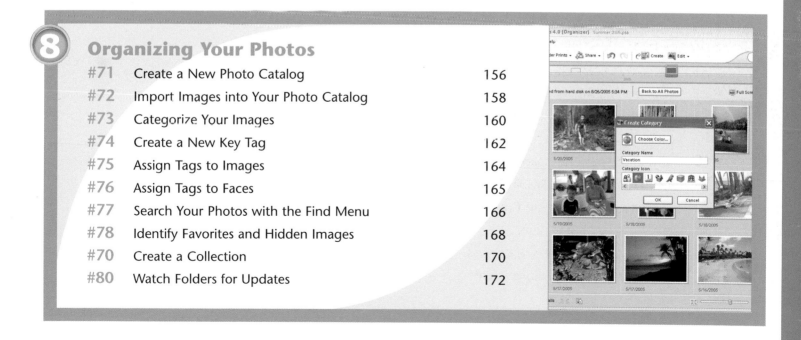

Table of Contents

Working with Layers and Selections

You can create, edit, and manipulate images and photos in many ways using Photoshop Elements 4. With the layers feature, for example, you can create floating canvases and combine them into a more complex image. Similar to a cartoon animation, a layered image lets you arrange the separate canvases in front of a background.

In Elements, you can adjust all of the objects on one layer without directly or permanently affecting the other layers. For example, you can move, transform, colorize, erase, or distort an individual layer. You can learn how to add special effects, use layers to change other layers, and even make objects semitransparent. This makes layers a very helpful feature for creating art and editing photos.

You can also achieve amazing effects with the selection tools and mask tools. Selection tools allow you to specify the areas or pixels you want to change by selecting them in the image. When you make a selection, you are telling the program to change only the selected pixels and no unselected pixels. The selection tool uses a moving dotted line, also called *marching ants*, to delineate the selected area.

Layers and selections are extremely useful when working with complex images. In this chapter, you will discover how to get the most out of these tools.

Top 100

Achieve transparency effects with the
OPACITY SETTING

You can give your photos an almost surreal look by adjusting the opacity of layers in your image. When you reduce the opacity of a layer, you are simply making it more transparent, allowing pixels beneath that layer to become visible. This semitransparency effect has some very creative uses. For example, you can apply it to text to make the words you choose more subtle, you can make an image semitransparent to show a second image below it,

and you can give shapes and layer objects an almost spectral appearance for backgrounds or image overlays.

You can change your opacity settings at any time. You can also use opacity to work with layers below an object while still being able to detect the boundaries of the object. This is very useful in images that have many layers with overlapping objects.

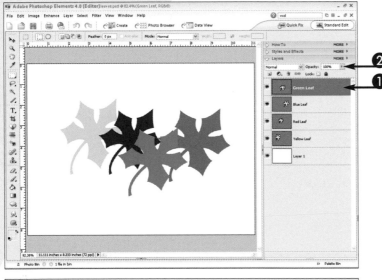

❶ In the Layers palette, click the layer you want to change.

❷ Click here to display the Opacity slider.

The Opacity slider appears.

❸ Click and drag the Opacity slider to set the percentage of opacity you want.

● The opacity of the layer you selected changes to the percentage you specified.

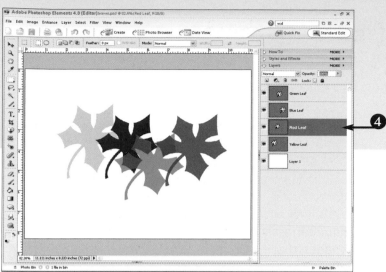

Alternatively, you can type a value between 0 and 100 in the Opacity field.

④ In the Layers palette, click the layer you want to change.

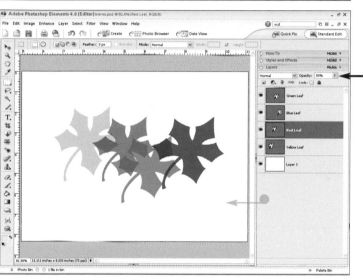

⑤ In the Opacity field, type the percentage of opacity you want.

● The opacity of the layer you selected changes to the percentage you specified.

TIPS

Did You Know?

You cannot change the opacity of a background layer unless you first transform it into a regular layer. Click Layer, New, and then Layer From Background. You can also double-click the background layer in the Layers palette; a prompt allows you to convert it to a regular layer.

Did You Know?

When you overlap the objects in two layers with lower opacity settings, the objects' opacity increases. Opacity is cumulative in multiple layers. For example, if you have a layer with a yellow circle and a layer with a blue circle, you can set both layers to 50% opacity and partially overlap the circles. The overlapping colors combine to create a more opaque green color.

Use the blending modes to
BLEND LAYERS

You can use Photoshop Elements' blending modes to create special effects in your layers. The blending modes take the pixels of a layer and cause them to interact with the pixels of another layer. This affects the hues, tones, and saturations of the lower layer.

Each blending mode defines how a layer interacts with other layers, mostly in the area of highlights, midtones, shadows, and color. For example, highlight-based filters ignore midtone and shadows

and adjust only the lighter-colored pixels. Shadow and midtone blending modes affect dark and midrange tones, respectively. The color modes affect only the hue, saturation, and color blends of the layer, leaving the contrast and tones unaffected.

Try experimenting with each blending mode. Each image has its own range of tones and color, and there is often no way to predict how each blending mode will affect the other layers.

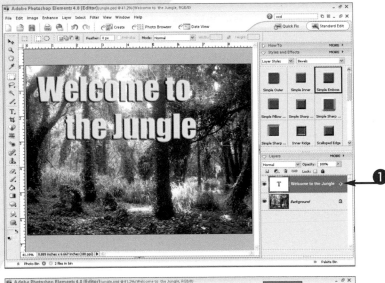

① In the Layers palette, click the layer you want to blend.

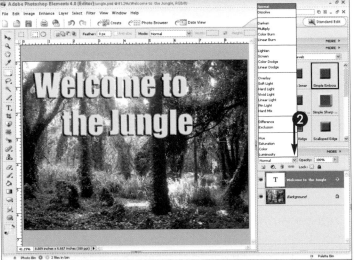

② Click here to open the Blending Modes menu.

DIFFICULTY LEVEL

● Elements blends the selected layer with the layers below it.

TIPS

Did You Know?

Blending modes are not permanent; you can reset and adjust them at any time. However, they do affect all layers below the layer you are modifying. When you adjust a layer effect, the pixels of all the layers below it are also affected. You can adjust the opacity to reduce the effects of the blending modes.

Did You Know?

You can use multiple blending mode layers to achieve many different effects. Blending modes are cumulative, meaning that if you have three layers and the middle layer has a blending mode, only the bottom layer is affected. If the top layer also had a blending mode, its blending mode would affect both the middle and bottom layers.

Chapter 1: Working with Layers and Selections

Work with
ADJUSTMENT LAYERS

You can alter the appearance of layers using other layers that have special properties. These special layers are called *adjustment layers*. Adjustment layers affect a specific property of the layers below them, such as hue/saturation, levels, or contrast.

Adjustment layers are versatile because they allow you to make dramatic changes to your original image without changing it irreversibly. For example, you can enhance image color or increase the contrast of faded photographs.

By default, an adjustment layer affects all layers below it. However, you can specify that an adjustment layer affect only one layer by grouping it with that layer.

You can use adjustment layers to make initial adjustments to digital camera imports or scans, or to correct improper color balance or poor contrast. The ability to change your images significantly without changing them permanently makes adjustment layers invaluable for photo corrections.

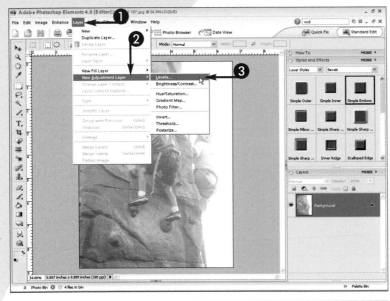

1 Click Layer.

2 Click New Adjustment Layer.

3 Click the category you want to adjust.

The New Layer dialog box appears.

4 Type a name for the new layer.

5 Click here and select a mode.

6 Click here and select an opacity percentage.

7 Click OK.

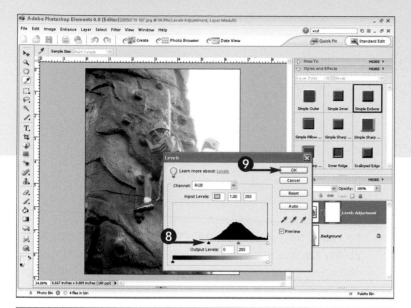

The Levels dialog box appears.

⑧ Click and drag the sliders to make adjustments.

⑨ Click OK.

Elements applies your settings.

Because the changes exist in the adjustment layer, the underlying layer remains intact.

TIPS

Did You Know?
You do not have to apply an adjustment layer to an entire image. You can create a selection and apply the adjustment only to that selection area. Simply select the area you want to change using a selection tool before you create your adjustment layer. You can lower the opacity of an adjustment layer to soften the effect.

Did You Know?
You can use adjustment layers to affect other adjustment layers. Adjustment layers are cumulative and affect not only the regular layers below them, but also the adjustment layers. For example, two color adjustment layers set at less than 100% opacity can complement each other, blending color effects and applying those effects to the underlying layers.

MOVE OBJECTS
in layers

You can take advantage of the flexibility of layers and the mobility of the objects they contain. Layers are useful because their content is independent of the content in other layers; what you do to one layer does not affect the others unless you intend it to.

You can place your layer objects wherever you want within the image boundaries. To adjust the position of your objects, you can use the Move tool.

Using the Move tool creates a bounding box around the individual object or objects within the layer. By clicking and dragging the object, you can place it where you want it. Alternatively, you can use the arrow keys on the keyboard for more precise positioning.

You can click a different object to select it, or click any layer in the Layers palette to switch the Move tool to a new layer.

You can also switch layers by right-clicking anywhere in the image when using the Move tool. Any layers that overlap where you click should appear in a list that you can choose from to select a layer.

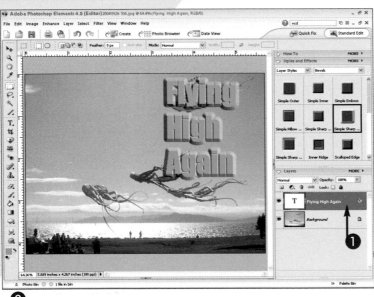

❶ In the Layers palette, click the layer that contains the object you want to move.

❷ Click the Move tool.

● By default, the Move tool automatically selects the objects in the currently selected layer.

3 1833 04884 122 2

③ Click and drag the object that you want to move to its new position.

DIFFICULTY LEVEL

The object moves without affecting the other layers.

Did You Know?

You can move multiple layers at once with the Move tool by first linking them together. To link layers, click one layer and then, in the Layers palette, click the empty box next to the Eye icon for any other layers you want to link. A chain appears denoting the link.

Shortcut Keys!

You can access the Move tool at almost any time by holding the Ctrl key while using another tool. Most tools allow you to use this shortcut. When you use the keyboard to move an object, holding the Shift key while pressing the arrow keys moves the object several pixels at a time instead of one pixel at a time.

ORGANIZE
layers

You can shuffle layers in your image to make it more visually appealing; this is possible with just a few mouse clicks in the Layers palette. Because layers are like sheets of paper, you can easily adjust the appearance of your image simply by moving a layer up or down in the Layers palette. Giving the layer a more descriptive name is also a good idea.

Each layer acts like a separate file; the changes you make to one layer do not affect other layers. However, some special effects, such as blending

modes, are designed to affect other layers. You can experiment to see how certain layers affect other layers.

You can move all the layers except the background layer. However, you can convert the background layer into a regular layer if you need to move it.

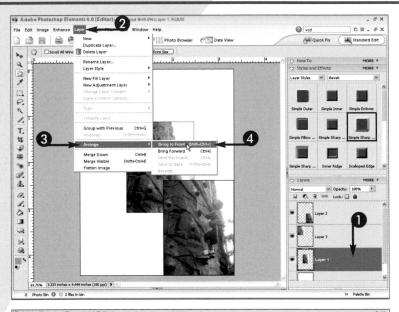

ORGANIZE LAYERS USING THE MENU

1. In the Layers palette, click the layer that you want to move to a different stacking order.

2. Click Layer.

3. Click Arrange.

4. Select an arrangement from the submenu.

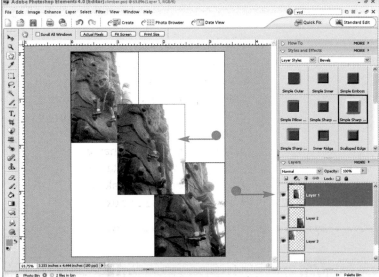

● The layers shuffle and appear in their new order.

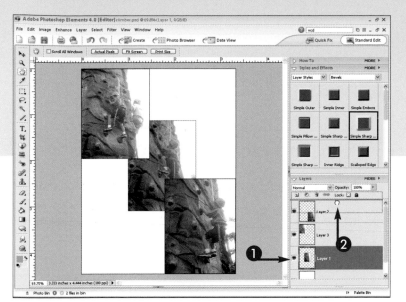

ORGANIZE LAYERS BY DRAGGING

1. In the Layers palette, click the layer that you want to move to a different stacking order.

2. Click and drag the layer to its new position.

DIFFICULTY LEVEL

● The layers shuffle and appear in their new order.

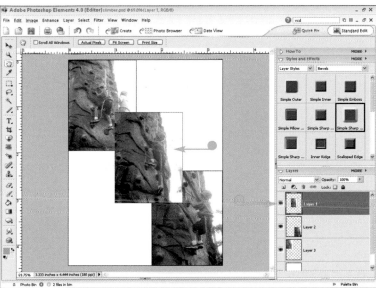

TIPS

Shortcut Keys!

You can take advantage of a few keyboard shortcuts to rearrange your layers.

Shortcuts	Function
Ctrl+]	Moves a layer up one level
Ctrl+[	Moves a layer down one level
Shift+Ctrl+]	Moves a layer to the front
Shift+Ctrl+[	Moves a layer to the back

Did You Know?

You can easily rename your layer. Click the layer you want to rename in the Layers palette, click Layer, and then click Rename Layer. In the Layer Properties dialog box, type a new name and click OK to rename the layer. You can also double-click the layer in the Layers palette to open the same dialog box.

Work with the
LASSO TOOL

You can make custom and complex selections with the Lasso tool. The Lasso tool allows you to draw any shape you want with your mouse, and that shape becomes the selection area. A boundary line appears where you click and drag your mouse. If you bring the mouse back to its origin, a small letter *o* appears next to the cursor, meaning the selection is enclosed. You can release the mouse button at this point. Marching ants appear, enclosing the area you have drawn. Releasing the cursor sooner causes the endpoint to connect to the origin with a straight line, also enclosing the selected area.

The Magnetic Lasso tool allows you to draw a complex selection that intuitively follows the shape of an object. For example, you can easily draw around any object, such as a person's face or a flower, and the Magnetic Lasso tool corrects your path to accurately surround the object. You can deselect your selection by clicking the mouse inside a completed selection.

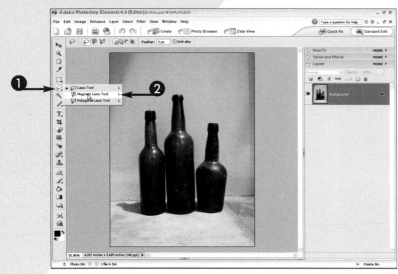

① Click and hold the cursor over the Lasso tool.

The Lasso tool selection bar appears.

② Select a Lasso tool.

This example uses the Magnetic Lasso tool.

③ Click and drag to make a selection.

④ Move the cursor back to the point of origin and release the mouse button.

With the Magnetic or Polygonal Lasso, a small letter *o* appears by the cursor when you reach the point of origin.

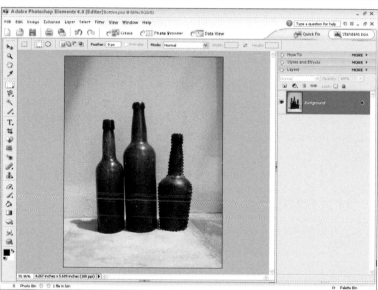

An active selection area appears, based on the boundaries you have drawn.

TIPS

Customize It!

You can add and delete parts of a selection after you complete it. To add to the current selection, press and hold down the Shift key while selecting the area you want to add. To subtract from the current selection, press and hold down the Alt key while selecting the area you want to subtract.

Did You Know?

You can save your selections for use later on. By clicking Select and then Save Selection, you can name and save your selection in the PSD image format. If you are using a different image format, Elements saves the selection until you close the image, at which time it is discarded.

Make selections with the
SELECTION BRUSH
tool

You can easily make selections with one of the most innovative selection tools Elements has to offer: the Selection Brush tool. This tool acts like the regular brush tool except that when you paint you are selecting that area rather than adding color. The Selection Brush tool gives you a quick, easy way to make oddly shaped selections.

When you use the Selection Brush tool, you can choose from the library of brush shapes. You simply

choose a brush and begin painting; the shape, size, and other options of that brush are all applied to the selection area.

You can adjust the hardness option to vary your brush edges from soft, or lightly feathered, to crisp. This replaces the feathering option that is available on most of the other selection tools. You can deselect a selection by clicking the mouse inside the selection.

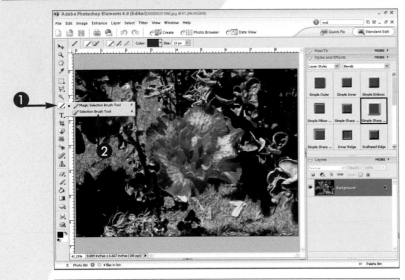

① Click and hold the Magic Selection Brush tool.

② Click the Selection Brush tool.

③ Click here and select a brush shape.

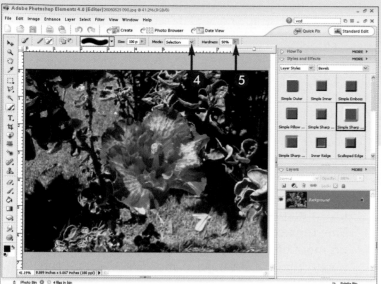

④ Click here and select Selection.

⑤ Click here and select the hardness percentage you want for the brush edges.

DIFFICULTY LEVEL

⑥ Click and drag with strokes to make a selection.

When making a selection, you can make multiple strokes by keeping your mouse pressed down.

![TIPS]

Did You Know?

You can erase areas of a drawing by pressing and holding the Alt key while drawing with the Selection Brush tool. This is a convenient way to correct mistakes when making a selection.

Did You Know?

You can alter the brush's settings or shape between brush strokes. You can also change any Options bar items you want. The Selection Brush tool uses these settings without affecting the settings of previously selected areas.

Did You Know?

You can choose Mask from the Mode drop-down menu in the Options bar. Masks create selections by painting over the areas you do not want to change. When you choose a different tool or return to Selection Mode, the mask becomes a normal selection.

Modify
your selections

You can adjust your selections after you complete them by changing their size, structure, and edges. For example, two of the most commonly used tools are Contract and Expand, which modify the size of your selections. These tools are both particularly useful for working with complex shapes.

You can alter the size of your selections with these tools. For example, the Contract tool moves the perimeter of your selection inward by a specified number of pixels. The new size is constrained and is proportional to the original. This is an excellent tool if you want to create an inner edge on an object.

The Expand tool is similar to the Contract tool except that it moves the perimeter of the selection outward. You can use the Expand tool to create an outline or to ensure that what you delete from an image leaves no remaining pixels. Both tools allow you to make adjustments, but excessive adjustments can cause the selection to lose its clarity.

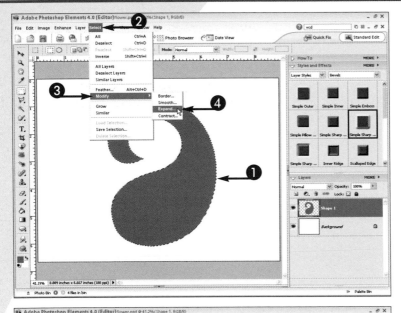

❶ Create a selection with a selection tool.

❷ Click Select.

❸ Click Modify.

❹ Click Expand.

The Expand Selection dialog box appears.

❺ Type a number by which you want to expand your selection in pixels.

❻ Click OK.

Elements expands the selection by the number of pixels you specified.

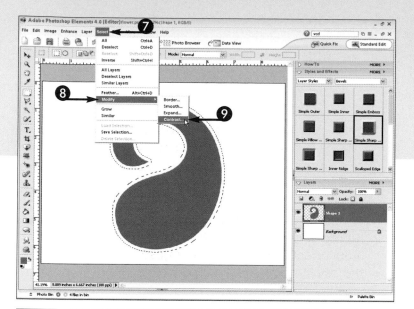

7 Click Select.

8 Click Modify.

9 Click Contract.

The Contract Selection dialog box appears.

10 Type a number by which you want to contract your selection in pixels.

11 Click OK.

Elements contracts the selection by the number of pixels you specified.

TIPS

Customize It!

You can manipulate selected areas with the Transform tool. Elements allows you to transform selections just as you can transform shapes and objects. For example, you can scale down and distort selections. The changes you make affect only the area within the selection, which can reduce processing time.

More Options!

You can easily invert your selections. After you make a selection, click Select and then Invert — or type Shift+Ctrl+I — and the selection changes from the area you originally selected to the area that was not selected. This is useful for deleting backgrounds from around an object.

COPY AND PASTE
with a selection tool

You can use the selection tools to copy and paste parts of an image. One of the most common uses for the selection tools is to copy a selection from one image or layer to another image or layer. You can use the different selection tools to cut out your subject and place that subject on another layer or even into another document.

Copying with a selection is simple. You can use any of the selection tools to create an outline around the subject. Elements does not recognize any part of the image outside of the selected area, so clicking Edit and then Copy copies only what is inside the selection boundaries. You can then simply create a new layer and paste the clipboard copy of your selection onto the new layer.

You can use selections to copy important parts of an image that you are about to edit. This lets you protect your image from permanent changes or create a specifically shaped selection for a special effect, such as a double image.

❶ Create a selection with a selection tool.

❷ Click Edit.

❸ Click Copy.

❹ Click inside the selection to deselect it.

❺ Click Layer.

❻ Click New.

❼ Click Layer.

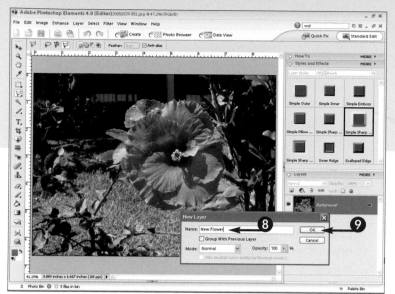

The New Layer dialog box appears.

8 Type a name for the new layer.

9 Click OK.

DIFFICULTY LEVEL

10 Click Edit.

11 Click Paste.

● Elements pastes the copied selection onto the new layer.

TIPS

Did You Know?
You can copy all the layers in an image when using selections. When you use the Copy command, you are only making a copy of the active layer. If you have a multilayered document, you can use the Copy Merged command to create a selection copy of *all* the layers.

Did You Know?
You can paste your copy in several different ways. For example, if you do not deselect your selection, you can paste the copy directly into the original selection area, on a new layer. If you deselect your selection, you can press and hold the Shift key while clicking Paste, and the object appears in the exact center of the document.

FEATHER
your selections

You can create selections with edges that are smooth and gradual. Feathering an edge causes the selection edges to become semitransparent, blending with the image behind the selection. Feathered edges are useful when copying and cutting selections from images. Feathering reduces stark, choppy edges, improving the overall appearance of the image.

Most selection tools have feathering options that you can specify before you make a selection, so the feathering option is built into your selection. If you

do not choose a feathering option or have already made a selection, you can use the Select menu to apply feathering.

You can use feathering when you are removing elements from one image and placing them into another. You can also use feathering to create framing effects, vignettes, and other edge effects. The value you enter in the Feather Selection dialog box controls the amount of blend and blur that are applied to the edges of the selection.

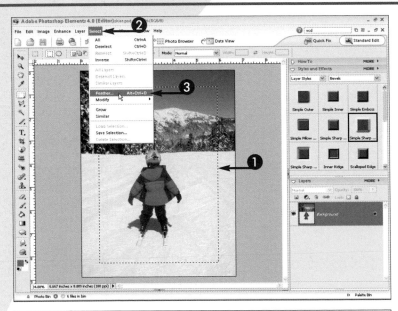

1 Create a selection with a selection tool.

2 Click Select.

3 Click Feather.

The Feather Selection dialog box appears.

4 Type a value in the Feather Radius box.

This value sets the amount of feathering.

5 Click OK.

Elements feathers your selection.

6 Click Select.

7 Click Inverse.

Elements inverts your selection.

DIFFICULTY LEVEL

8 Press Delete.

Elements deletes the area that was not selected.

● You can now see the effect of the feathering.

TIPS

Did You Know?
You can use the Feather option to remove objects from layers. However, you should leave a slight buffer of pixels around a selected object so that you do not erase or blur its edges.

Did You Know?
You can feather your selections and still apply layer styles to the selected objects. Layer styles recognize most of the pixels within the feathered edge and apply the filter to them. The result may appear semitransparent because of the feathering, but the styles can still enhance your graphics.

Shortcut Keys!
Elements lets you use shortcuts when making selections. Ctrl+Shift+I selects the inverse of an active selection, Ctrl+D deselects any current selections, and Ctrl+Shift+D reselects the last selection you made.

Creative Designing with Filters and Effects

Photoshop Elements 4 has a wide range of filters that you can use to add incredible special effects to your images. Although the information about filters could fill an entire book, this chapter explores their more interesting features. Filters range from simple blurs to techniques that mimic artistic painting styles. For example, you can use distortions, sketch strokes, and textures to transform an ordinary image into an extraordinary one.

Many filters have adjustments and settings that can completely change the final result. You can also apply filters on top of other filters to create new effects. It is important to remember that when you apply filters, you may permanently change the layer object or image. As a result, you should consider making a duplicate of your image before applying a filter.

In addition to filters, Elements contains a large selection of effects that you can apply to your images, shapes, and text. You can use effects that do everything from giving your image a brick wall appearance to replicating popular photographic techniques. As with filters and layer styles, you can apply effects from a palette to enhance your photographs and layered images, taking them from plain to dynamic.

Top 100

Create an
OLD NEWSPAPER PHOTO EFFECT

You can transform your full-color photographs to resemble old newspaper photographs. This process uses the Reticulation and Equalize filters to create a black-and-white dot-style photograph, which resembles the old newsprint photographic style. This is a neat effect for family photographs and Web page design.

The Reticulation filter simulates a photo development technique that causes the ink to merge into dots instead of a smooth finish. The Equalize filter finds the lightest and darkest tones in the image, and evenly spreads all of the remaining tones between

them. This helps to create a more neutral tone for the final result. You can occasionally end up with a strong grainy effect on your image, depending on the level of these two filters you apply. You can use the Blur filters to help smooth out the rougher pixelization to enhance the newspaper photograph effect.

It is best to work from larger original photographs with the Reticulation filter in order to retain the details in the image. Smaller images can lose detail, especially photographs with finer features, such as those with human faces.

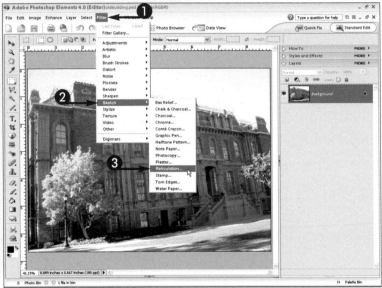

① Click Filter.

② Click Sketch.

③ Click Reticulation.

The Reticulation dialog box appears.

④ Click and drag the sliders to adjust the reticulation settings.

⑤ Click OK.

Elements applies the Reticulation filter to the image.

6 Click Filter.

7 Click Adjustments.

8 Click Equalize.

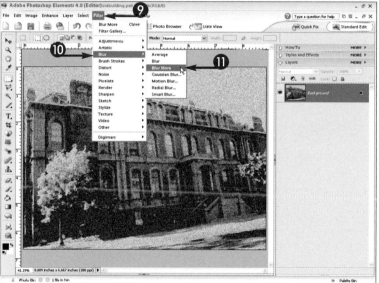

Elements applies the Equalize filter to the image.

9 Click Filter.

10 Click Blur.

11 Click Blur More.

Elements applies the Blur More filter, eliminating some of the graininess of the image.

You can repeat the Blur More steps to further reduce image graininess.

TIPS

Customize It!

You can create a color newspaper photograph effect. To do this, first duplicate the original image layer. Select the original layer and perform the steps in this task. Select the duplicate layer, and position it above the original layer in the Layers palette. Change the duplicate image's blending mode to Color. The photo now looks like a color newspaper image.

Did You Know?

You can create the illusion of age with the newspaper effect. Newspapers fade with age. After you complete the newspaper effect in steps **1** to **11**, click Filters, then Adjustments, and then Photo Filter. Apply a Sepia or similar color tone to create a yellowed newspaper effect. See Task #39 for more information.

Turn your photo into an
ARTIST'S SKETCH

You can change your favorite picture into a drawing. By using the Elements 3 filters, you can make an ordinary photograph look like an artist's sketch, a trick that you can perform with almost any image. You can apply this feature to create coloring books and trace patterns.

You can achieve a variety of sketch effects using different options in the Filter menu to stylize your photograph. For example, some popular sketch filters include Conte Crayon, Charcoal, and Graphic Pen. You can achieve even more unusual sketch effects by

applying one sketch filter on top of another. You should experiment to discover which of these artistic filters work best for you.

The purpose for using the Enhance tool in this task is to desaturate, or remove, the colors from the image. You can also use the Enhance menu to manually adjust the levels of the image, which increases the clarity of the shapes within the image. Reducing the depth of the photo with these tools makes the Find Edges filter more accurate because the edges are clearly defined.

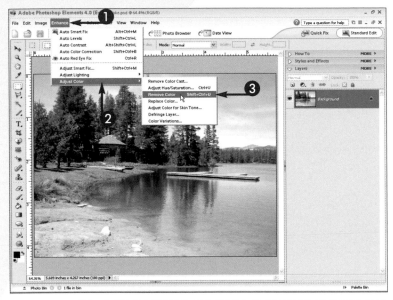

① Click Enhance.

② Click Adjust Color.

③ Click Remove Color.

Elements converts your image to black and white.

④ Click Enhance.

⑤ Click Auto Levels.

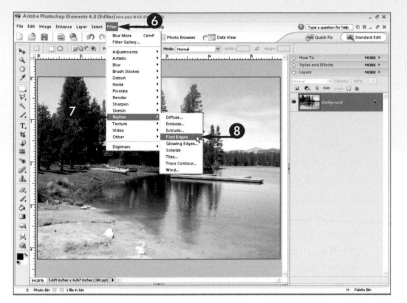

Elements increases the contrast and brightness of your image.

⑥ Click **Filter**.

⑦ Click **Stylize**.

⑧ Click **Find Edges**.

12

DIFFICULTY LEVEL

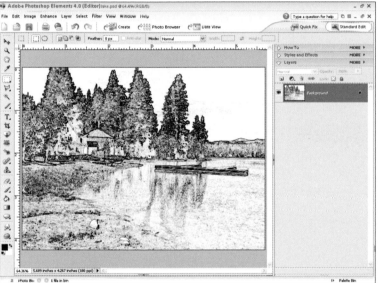

Elements applies the Find Edges filter and creates a pencil sketch.

TIP

Customize It!

You can retain some color in your sketch by skipping the desaturation steps — steps **1** to **3** — in this task. When you do this, Elements creates a colored pencil sketch effect in your final image.

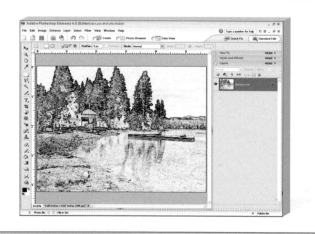

Remove grain and noise to
SHARPEN A PHOTO

You can improve a photograph's clarity and detail by correcting a blurry image. By using Element's sharpening tools, you can restore some of the crispness of the original photograph. One of the most powerful tools in Elements for restoring crispness is the Unsharp Mask filter.

When you apply too much sharpening to an image, this can result in excessive noise. The Unsharp Mask filter can solve this problem by giving you excellent control when balancing between clarity and noise.

This filter is unique among the sharpening tools because you are able to specify exactly how the pixels are affected during the sharpening process.

The Unsharp Mask filter uses three options that affect the sharpening process: Amount, Radius, and Threshold. The *Amount* option specifies how much sharpening you want, the *Radius* option defines the thickness of the resulting edges, and the *Threshold* option specifies the relative difference in contrast that must exist between pixels before they are affected. Together, these three options allow you to get the best results when sharpening your photograph or image.

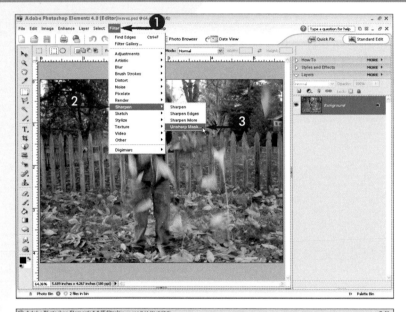

① Click Filter.

② Click Sharpen.

③ Click Unsharp Mask.

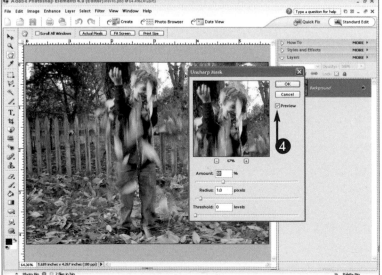

The Unsharp Mask dialog box appears.

A full image preview displays in the dialog box.

④ Click the Preview check box (☐ changes to ☑).

The main document reflects your changes immediately.

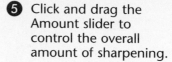

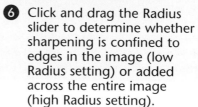

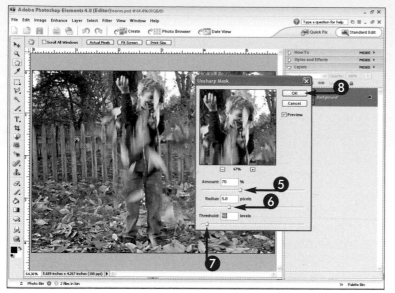

5 Click and drag the Amount slider to control the overall amount of sharpening.

6 Click and drag the Radius slider to determine whether sharpening is confined to edges in the image (low Radius setting) or added across the entire image (high Radius setting).

7 Click and drag the Threshold slider to control how much contrast must be present for an edge to be recognized and sharpened.

Each setting affects the other, so further adjustments may be necessary.

8 Click OK.

Elements applies the Unsharp Mask to sharpen the photo.

TIPS

Caution!

The results of the Unsharp Mask filter are very dramatic at higher settings. Before applying the filter, you should look at several different parts of the image in the Image Preview to ensure that there is not too much noise or degradation in quality. It is recommended that you use a duplicate of the original until you are completely satisfied with the results.

Customize It!

You can use the Unsharp Mask filter on both selections and layer objects. By creating your selection or selecting a specific layer, you can apply the Unsharp Mask to a specific area in your image. This is very useful when you are incorporating photo objects into a separate image, where the difference in clarity is noticeable.

Turn your photos into
WATERCOLOR ART

You can use Artistic filters to transform a photograph into a different medium to look as if it were painted with oils or watercolors. You can also use a variety of filters in different combinations to create different strokes and textures. The simplicity with which you can convert an image to art is amazing, and the effects are easy to change. You should play with the different artistic and brush stroke filter styles to see what kinds of media you can imitate.

You can replicate a realistic watercolor style using the Watercolor filter, which mimics the soft, saturated edges and colors of an actual watercolor painting. After a second repetition of the filter to emphasize the style, you can apply the Dry Brush filter to create the random strokes of brushes on a canvas.

Adding textures to the results can mimic the effect of a canvas to complete the illusion of an actual oil or acrylic painting. It is best to experiment to learn the subtleties of these filters.

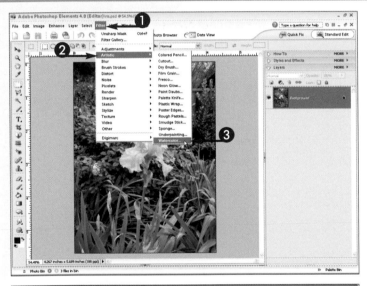

① Click Filter.

② Click Artistic.

③ Click Watercolor.

The Filter Browser appears, displaying the Watercolor option.

④ Click and drag the sliders to adjust your watercolor settings.

Elements applies the Watercolor filter in the Preview window.

⑤ Click OK to apply one filter.

● You can click here to insert another filter layer.

If you want a more pronounced effect, repeat steps **1** to **5** to apply Watercolor a second time.

⑥ In the Filter Browser's Artistic menu, click Dry Brush.

⑦ Click and drag the sliders to adjust your dry brush settings.

⑧ Click OK.

Elements applies the Dry Brush filter.

TIPS

Put It Together!

You can take a photograph that you have converted to a watercolor image and frame it by using the steps in Task #15. This combination allows you to create fully framed artwork that you can mount on a wall or send online to family and friends.

Customize It!

To obtain a more abstract effect in this task, you can click Filter, Artistic, and then Cutout filter in steps **1** to **3**. You can also click Image, Adjustments, and then Posterize, or apply one of the Blur filters to reduce the amount of fine detail in the original photograph.

FRAME
your photographic images

You can quickly and easily create a group of framed photographs for your digital photo albums and other graphics projects in Elements 4. Photograph frames are an excellent way to present your photographs in a website or personal project.

You can create a frame by using the Stroke command, which draws pixels in relation to a selection's boundary. There are several options that you can adjust to change this effect. You can then use layer styles to give the frame a more customized look.

You can also create a frame using the built-in frame effects in the Effects menu. You can use these quick and easy frame styles to enhance the appearance of your photographs with a wide variety of effects, including wood, plastic, brushed metal, and photograph corner tab designs. You can also use multiple frame effects to create more-complex framing designs. You can use a vignette effect on an image, and then apply a wood frame to create a matted photograph effect. Experiment with different combinations to see what results you can design.

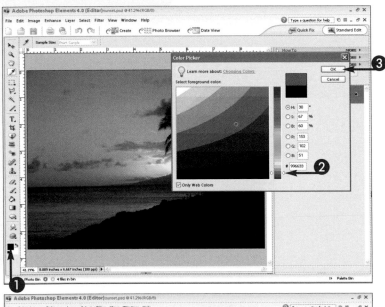

❶ Click the Foreground Color box.

The Color Picker dialog box appears.

❷ Click and drag the slider to set the foreground color.

❸ Click OK.

● Elements sets the new foreground color.

❹ Click here and click Effects.

The Effects palette appears.

5 Click here and click Frames.

6 Click a Frame Effect.

7 Click here to open the Effects Palette options menu.

8 Click Apply.

● Elements automatically adds a frame around your image.

TIPS

Customize It!

If a layer contains a layer style, then you can adjust the layer styles for that layer by double-clicking the *f* icon ( ). A dialog box appears, allowing you to adjust the layer effects.

Caution!

You can use many of the frame effects without altering your original image. However, some frames directly affect your image, and after you save the file, you cannot undo these changes. To prevent accidentally ruining the original, use these effects on a duplicate of your image.

Did You Know?

You can double-click on your selected Effect to apply it to your image without using the Options menu. This is a useful shortcut when working with effects in which you are familiar.

Design custom effects with the
COOKIE CUTTER TOOL

You can create some very exciting designs with the new Cookie Cutter tool. While this is not an actual effect from the Effects palette, the results from this tool are as creative and dynamic as any other effect. The Cookie Cutter tool uses Elements' Custom Shapes palette to create an automatic cutout of an image in the shape that you select from the menu.

You can select any shape from the Custom Shapes menu and click and drag it to any size and proportion you want. Elements uses that shape to create a

temporary mask that reveals only where the shape is, and discards the pixels outside the shape edges. You can adjust and move the shape tool to fine-tune the placement of the shape over the image. After you commit the Cookie Cutter shape, all other pixels are removed, and your shaped image appears on its own layer on a transparent background. This is an excellent way to design creative images quickly, replacing the traditional selection, cut, and paste methods.

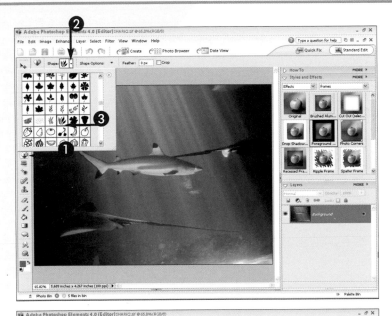

① Click the Cookie Cutter tool.

② Click here to open the Custom Shape palette.

③ Click a Custom Shape.

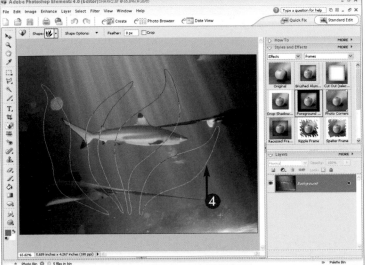

④ Click and drag the tool to create the shape you selected.

The shape draws outward from the point of origin to the direction in which you are dragging the mouse.

To constrain the shape to equal proportions, you can press and hold the Shift key while dragging.

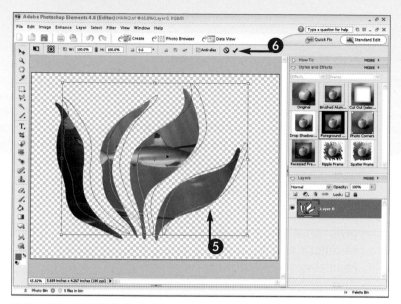

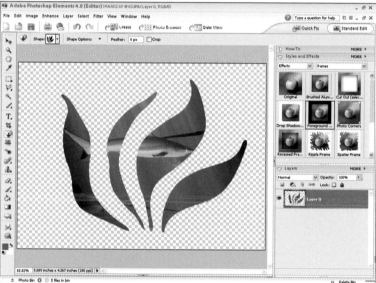

The area outside the shape becomes transparent.

⑤ Click and drag inside the bounding box to reposition the shape.

⑥ Click here to commit the change.

Elements applies the Cookie Cutter tool.

Elements discards the surrounding pixels.

TIPS

Try This!

The Cookie Cutter tool is excellent for scrapbook design. By using different shapes for your images, you can create unique looks that you can print on custom paper and place in your scrapbook projects. This is a fantastic way to creatively shape your images for holiday cards and other projects, as well.

Did You Know?

You can check online for additional Photoshop resources that have extra shapes available for download. You can save these shapes in the C:/Program Files/Adobe/Photoshop Elements 4.0/Presets/Custom Shapes folder. You can then load the shapes into your Shapes palette the next time you start Elements.

CREATE A SNOWSTORM
in your image

Elements has a fun effect that allows you to make it snow in your images at anytime, anywhere, and on anyone. You can use the Blizzard effect in the Effects palette to generate a realistic-looking scene of falling snow. The Blizzard effect uses a preset combination of filters and tools to add snow to your winter photos, or even to make it snow on the beach.

This effect does not change the original image or selection. Instead, Elements creates a separate layer, generates the blizzard, and sets the layer-blending mode to Screen. The Screen blending mode ignores the midtones and shadows of the blended layer, and accentuates the highlights, or in this case, the white snow. If you do not like the effect, you can make the layer invisible or delete it altogether without affecting your original image. In addition, because Elements recognizes the combination of filters and tools to create most Effects as a single step, you can undo the Blizzard effect simply by clicking the Undo button, allowing for fast reversal of undesired effects.

❶ Open your image or make a selection.

❷ Click here and click Effects.

The Effects palette appears.

❸ Click here and click Image Effects.

Elements' image effects appear.

❹ Click Blizzard.

5 Click here to open the Effects palette options menu.

6 Click Apply.

Elements applies the Blizzard effect.

Customize It!

You can make an even heavier snowstorm in your image. Select your image layer and apply the Blizzard effect a second time. Running the effect again creates another snow layer, doubling the effect of the snow. Because the Blizzard effect creates a random snow pattern each time, it makes the storm look fiercer, rather than having duplicate snow patterns.

Apply It!

You can make it snow inside a home or other impossible place. Find a photograph that contains a large window to a summer morning or an open door leading to a visible room inside the home. Make a selection, based on the windowpanes or the open door, and apply the Blizzard effect to it. You can also double-click the Blizzard icon to apply the effects.

Create a
WATER REFLECTION

You can flip text and apply a wavy effect to the letters, simulating a reflection on water. With the Water Reflection effect, Elements has taken a popular text effect and turned it into an easy trick, allowing you to add text reflections to paintings, photographs, and drawings.

You can generate a text layer and apply the Water Reflection effect. Elements duplicates the text as if it were reflected in front of the actual text, matching the color of the text you created. To make the

reflection more realistic, you can add a layer style to the text. This results in a more stylized reflection.

Like the other Text effects, you can only apply the Water Reflection effect to unsimplified text layers. These Text effects do not work on regular images, selections, or simplified objects. You can apply any Text Warp style before applying your Text Effects for more variety. Because creating warped text does not simplify the text layer, Text Effects like the Water Reflection will work with warped text.

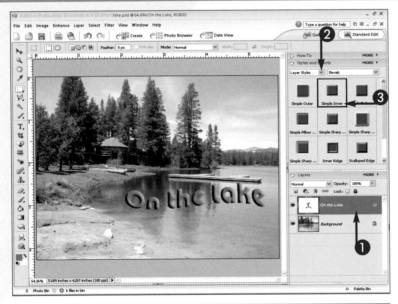

❶ Create a text layer.

❷ Click here and click Layer Styles.

❸ Click a style.

You can adjust the layer style settings to get the desired effect.

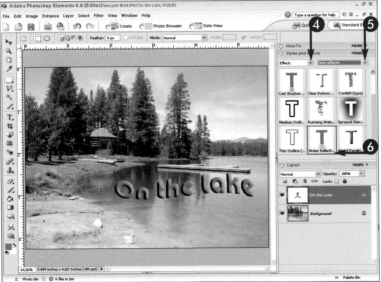

❹ Click here and click Effects.

The Effects palette appears.

❺ Click here and click Text Effects.

❻ Click Water Reflection.

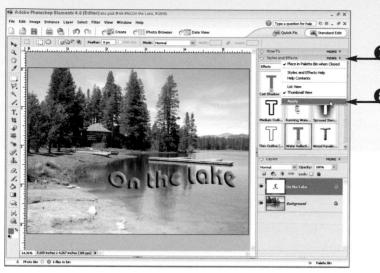

7 Click here to open the Effects palette options menu.

8 Click Apply.

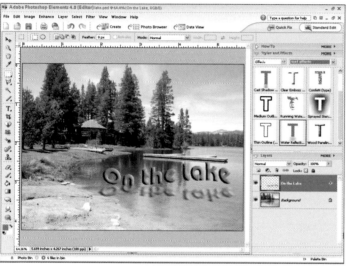

Elements applies the effect.

TIPS

Customize It!

You can apply any layer style or text effect before applying the Water Reflection effect, as long as it does not simplify the text layer. For example, you can use the Text Warp tool to apply a Flag or Bloat distortion, and then apply the Water Reflection effect. After the text layer is simplified, the Text effects do not work.

Caution!

After you apply a Text effect, Elements simplifies your text layer, and you can no longer edit it or change the font, size, or color. Test these effects on duplicate layers of your text, or apply these effects last, so that you can go back into the Undo History menu and undo them. After you save, the effect is permanent.

Make a
RUBBER STAMP

You can create a personal mark that you can use like a rubber stamp on your images. The Rubber Stamp effect creates a square-edged stamp out of whatever image you choose. High-quality, high-resolution images, such as complex photographs, may not make good stamps, because during the conversion process, their colors are flattened and posterized to a single color, which can ruin the details. You can use high-quality photographs, however, make sure that image size is as large as possible to retain as much detail as you can in the result. Gradients also do not

survive this effect very well. As a result, you should keep your original image simple in colors and design.

You can use the Rubber Stamp effect and convert the result into a custom brush. This is very handy for personal marks on copyright-protected images or digital documents. By defining the image as a brush, you can use it in any document that you create in Elements, or even create a small image that you can insert into a word-processing document or spreadsheet.

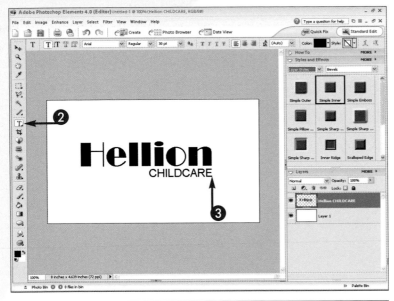

① Open a new document.

② Click the Type tool.

③ Click inside the image and type your text.

You can apply warps or adjustments to the text.

④ Click here and click Effects.

The Effects palette appears.

⑤ Click here and click Image Effects.

⑥ Double-click the Rubber Stamp effect.

● If you are prompted to merge the layers, click OK.

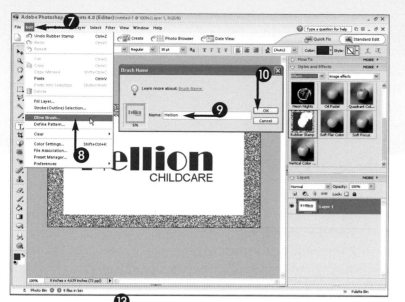

7 Click Edit.

8 Click Define Brush.

The Brush Name dialog box appears.

9 Type a name for the brush.

10 Click OK.

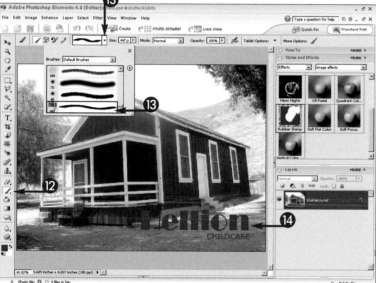

11 Open an image.

12 Click the Brush tool.

13 Click here and click the Stamp brush from the menu.

14 Click in the image.

The rubber stamp appears on the image.

TIPS

Customize It!

You can save your rubber stamp in various sizes. Before you apply the Rubber Stamp effect, duplicate your image and resize it. Apply the rubber stamp to the resized image. By resizing several duplicates of your image, you can create variable rubber stamp sizes that you can use in almost any size of document or image. This helps you to avoid resizing applied brushes, which results in pixelated edges and loss of clarity.

Did You Know?

Even though the Rubber Stamp tool applies the stamp in red, the brush always defaults to the foreground color that you select when using it, unless your image is in grayscale mode. You can also affect the opacity, as with any brush, for a more subtle effect.

BLUR THE BACKGROUND
to make an image stand out

You can use the Blur tool to make an object the center of attention. The Blur tool results in a loss of focus, drawing attention away from the content to which it is applied. For example, some images have a subject that can become lost in the detail surrounding it. Professional photographers use many different camera filters to obtain a blurred edge to frame their subject. You can use filters and selections to recreate this effect, mimicking the vignette blur filter used with cameras.

You can select the object that you want as the focus of the image, and blur everything else around it. How much and in what manner you blur around the object can also define the mood of the final image. This method, described as Department of Field in professional photography, is dynamic and works well on active subjects. Blurring the surroundings is a very easy and effective method of focusing attention on a specific subject.

❶ Select an area of your image using a selection tool.

❷ Click Select.

❸ Click Inverse.

❹ Click Filter.

❺ Click Blur.

❻ Click Radial Blur.

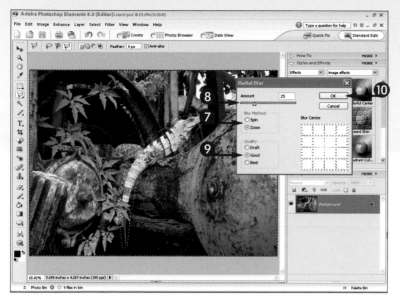

The Radial Blur dialog box appears.

⑦ Click a Blur Method (○ changes to ⊙).

⑧ Click and drag the Amount slider to adjust the setting.

⑨ Click a Quality setting (○ changes to ⊙).

⑩ Click OK.

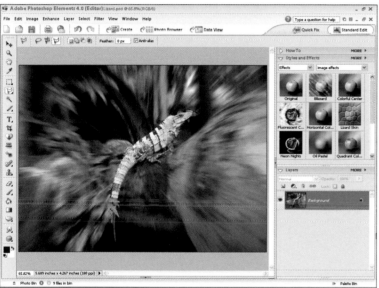

Elements applies the Radial Blur.

To turn off your selection, you can click Select and then Deselect from the menu.

TIPS

Customize It!

You can create different effects by adjusting your selection area. For example, when making your initial selection, feather the edges, so that when you apply the Blur effect, it blends smoothly with the unaffected section. In addition, while using symmetrical shapes can add more focus to an object, custom selections are better for complex subjects, such as people and animals.

Customize It!

The type and amount of blur that you use also affects your result. For example, using the Zoom filter adds a dynamic effect to the results, while using the Gaussian blur creates a softer effect, allowing the subject to create the mood. You can also try using the motion blur to generate a directional movement that accents active subjects.

Mastering Type, Brushes, and Shapes

The fact that you are working in Photoshop Elements 4 does not mean that you are limited to working with just photographs. On the contrary, you have a wide variety of tools at your disposal. Not only can you work with photographs in Elements, but you can also take advantage of a variety of cool features, such as text, brushes, and shapes.

Adding type is particularly useful when you want to create a Web page, add a caption, or simply label or headline your photograph. Simply create your text, and you can now jazz it up with patterns, styles, and special effects, such as beveling and drop shadows.

Text is not the only special tool at your disposal. In Elements, you can use custom brushes to personalize your photos or Web pages. Elements offers 12 sets of brushes for you to choose from, and you have the option of creating your own custom brushes. Whatever your artistic skill level, drawing with brushes is exciting.

You can also add special effects to your photographs, and use them as buttons on your Web page. For example, just as you can add three-dimensional effects to text, you can bevel your photographs in the same way, creating buttons that seem to "pop out" at your Web page visitors. You can also create custom shapes.

Fortunately, customizing Elements is not difficult — it is just a matter of knowing the proper steps to take, which you can learn in this chapter.

Top 100

Create
SEMITRANSPARENT TEXT

You can adjust the Opacity setting of your text layer to achieve semitransparent text. When an object is *semitransparent*, you can see objects and pixels that lay directly behind it. By making text semitransparent, you are able to view what is behind it while still being able to read the text.

Semitransparent text is a popular design element in graphics; it lends subtlety to the text, and depth to the image. Usually, it is not the focus of the image, but an extra design element that enhances or draws attention to the message that the image is conveying. For example, fully opaque text can dominate an image and draw attention away from the subject of the image. When you use semitransparent text, you can create a better balance between the text and the image.

You can apply the semitransparent effect to text that you have created with the Type tool. When you use the various Type tools, your text appears on its own layer, which allows you to work with the text without affecting the underlying image.

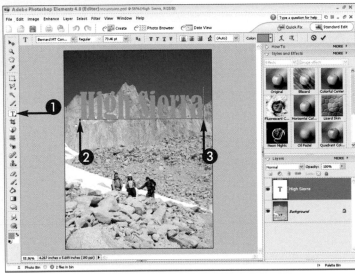

① Click the Type tool.

② Click where you want to place the text.

③ Type the text you want and press Enter.

You can change the text options by clicking a drop-down menu and making a selection.

④ In the Layers palette, click the Text layer.

⑤ Click here to display the Opacity slider.

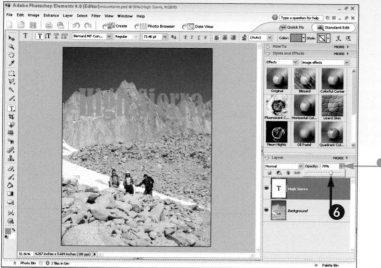

The Opacity slider appears.

6 Click and drag the Opacity slider to adjust the transparency level.

The text layer becomes more or less transparent, depending on where you drag the slider.

● Alternatively, you can type a value between 0 and 100 in the Opacity field and press Enter.

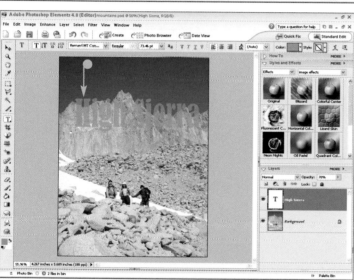

● Your semitransparent text appears in the photo.

TIPS

Did You Know?
You can change the opacity of semitransparent text without affecting the image. Keep in mind that you can always re-adjust it to suit your needs, and as long as the text layer remains difficult, you can edit the text attributes or content as well.

Did You Know?
You can also apply layer styles to a semitransparent text layer. Semi-transparency affects the entire layer and all applied effects. As a result, if you have applied layer styles to a text layer, and then change it to semitransparent text, the layer styles also become semitransparent.

Add
TEXT PATTERNS

In addition to applying layer styles, colors, and effects, you can also use text patterns as a design element to define and give character to your text. Patterns consist of repetitive graphics such as shapes, colors, or even clips of an image. Using patterns is an excellent way to emphasize the word content or complement surrounding graphics in your design.

A pattern fill always generates a new layer, and you can choose from one of three options when you

create a pattern fill: you can design a pattern as a full-sized layer design, apply it to a selection, or group it with a layer. Although grouping with a pattern layer may require that a full-sized layer be filled with the pattern, this pattern is only applied to the grouped objects. For example, with a text layer, only the text shows the pattern. With grouping, you can apply a pattern to any shape or text, and it does not cover anything but that shape or text.

① In the Layers palette, click the Text layer.

② Click Layer.

③ Click New Fill Layer.

④ Click Pattern.

The New Layer dialog box appears.

⑤ Type a name for your text layer.

⑥ Select Group With Previous Layer (☐ changes to ☑).

Selecting Group With Previous Layer constrains the pattern to the text.

⑦ Click OK.

The Pattern Fill dialog box appears.

8 Click here to display the sample patterns.

9 Select the pattern you want to apply.

10 Click here to scale the pattern within the text.

11 Click OK.

The new pattern appears within the text.

Did You Know?

Photoshop Elements comes with a variety of fill patterns in addition to the ones you see when you first open the Pattern Fill dialog box. To access more patterns, click the right arrow button from the window that pops up when selecting a pattern. Categories of patterns include Artist Surfaces, Nature Patterns, and more.

Put It Together!

You can really spice up your text by applying other special effects, such as type effects that make the text appear three-dimensional. Click the Layer Styles palette, select Bevels from the drop-down menu, and apply a bevel effect to your patterned text. Be careful of which layer styles you use, as some styles have built-in patterns that may erase the existing pattern.

Apply
TYPE MASKS

You can use the Type Mask tools to create selections in the shape of your text. Type masking is a feature that you can use to create custom selections using the font and font attributes that you select.

Type masking refers to the method in which you create these selections. As you type your text, it appears on a semitransparent red background as red cutout letters. This allows you to clearly see the area over which you are creating the selection, as well as allowing you better definition of the text and its attributes.

There are two types of Type Mask tools: horizontal and vertical. You can use the Horizontal Type Mask tool to create text selections with text appearing from left to right. You can use the Vertical Type Mask tool to create text selections with letters appearing below the preceding letter instead of to the right. These tools are similar to the regular and vertical Type tools. You can affect the masked text with any normal text tool options.

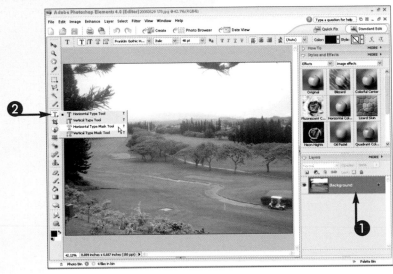

① In the Layers Palette, click a layer.

② Click the Type tool and then click the Horizontal Type Mask tool.

To create vertical text, click the Vertical Type Mask tool.

③ Click where you want to place the text.

The screen turns red, indicating that the text is masked.

④ Type the text you want.

The text you are typing does not appear in red. Instead, you can see the background image through the letters.

⑤ When you are finished typing, click the Commit Text button, or click a different tool.

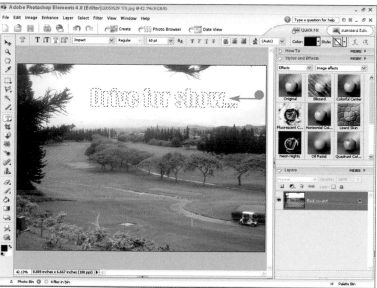

● Your masked text becomes a selection. The text appears as see-through type with dotted lines surrounding it.

TIPS

Did You Know?

Type masks are only editable while being created. After you commit the text, you can no longer edit it as you can a regular text layer. To alter the attributes of your text mask, you must change the attributes and retype the text as a new Type mask.

Did You Know?

As with other selection tools, holding the Shift key while committing either of the Type Mask tools will add the text selection to any existing selections. Holding the Alt key while committing will subtract the new selection area from any existing selections. This function is useful for creating multiple lines of text selections.

Change
TEXT ATTRIBUTES

You can change many attributes of your text, such as color, size, alignment, style, and font. *Font* refers to the unique standard width, weight, and style of the text. You can also affect the spacing between text lines, referred to as the leading.

It is best to change these attributes after you select the Type tool, and before you start typing. However, if you type your text and then decide that you want to change its appearance, you can still do so, as long as the Type tool is active. You can even change

specific parts of the text — such as certain letters or words — by selecting them with the Type tool.

In addition, there are several *faux* options available, including faux italic, bold, strikethrough, and underline. These options are available in the Type tool Options bar. They are especially useful when you are using a font that has no built-in italic or bold font styles. You can also apply the Warp Text tool, which enables you to alter the overall shape of the text.

① In the Layers palette, select a Type layer.

② Click the Type tool.

If you want the changes to apply only to certain parts of the text, highlight those letters or words.

③ Click here and select a style.

④ Click here and select a font.

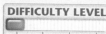

⑤ Click here and select a type size.

● You can also type a value for a specific font size.

● You can click here to set the leading value, or vertical space between the text rows.

Your formatting changes appear on-screen.

TIPS

Did You Know?

You can make the edges of your text appear smoother by using *anti-aliasing*. Anti-aliasing is a feature that you can turn on to improve the appearance of your type. To turn on this feature, click the Anti-Aliased button, located in the Type Options bar, next to the Font Size drop-down menu. It is denoted by two lowercase *a*'s.

Did You Know?

You can add new fonts to Elements by installing them on your computer. Elements draws all of its available fonts from your computer's default C:\Windows\Fonts folders. Be careful when sharing PSD files with text. If your destination computer does not have the font installed, Elements uses the closest substitution available in the existing font sets, which can change the effect.

Add effects with
LAYER STYLES

You can improve the appearance of your layers by using layer styles. Styles enable you to add dimension and special effects to objects in your image. You can apply styles to any layer except for the Background layer. When you apply styles to the Background layer, you are prompted to convert it to a regular layer so that Elements can apply the styles.

Elements offers 14 layer style categories, and you can apply these styles with a simple mouse click. Clicking more than one style can combine a new style with the current style or replace the current style completely.

Basic styles, such as bevels, shadows, and glow effects, have specific uses. Complex styles incorporate these basic styles, as well as patterns, color overlays, and other extras, to create unusual and original effects.

You can still edit text and shapes after you apply styles. Unlike most filters, styles can apply to vector graphics such as text and shapes without first requiring simplification. This is very useful if you want to perform editing and corrections later.

❶ In the Layers palette, click the layer to which you want to apply a style.

❷ Click here to open the Styles and Effects palette.

❸ Click Layer Styles.

● The Layer Styles palette opens.

❹ Click here and select a category.

The Layer Styles palette shows the category you selected.

⑤ Click the layer style you want to apply.

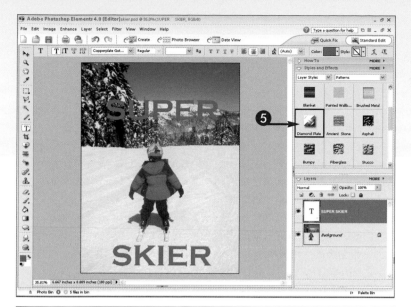

Elements applies the layer style.

● The *f* icon (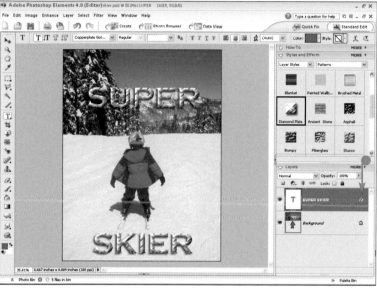) appears in the layer, indicating that you have applied a layer style.

DIFFICULTY LEVEL

TIPS

Did You Know?

You can remove all layer styles from a layer by right-clicking on the layer in the Layer Styles palette. Select Clear Layer Style from the pop-up menu to completely remove the style. Clearing the style can only be undone in the History palette. Click Window, then click Undo History to access this palette.

Customize It!

You can edit certain aspects of your layer styles. To do this, click the *f* icon ( ) in the Layers palette on the layer to which you have applied a style. A dialog box appears, enabling you to adjust your active style effects. You can change the settings on the active style effects and create a custom layer style for your project.

Design your own
CUSTOM BRUSHES

You can choose from hundreds of brushes to do your artwork and designs in Photoshop Elements. You can easily access a wide variety of shapes, designs, and styles through the Brushes palette. Elements allows you to create custom brushes when you want a different design or size of brush for a specific project. For example, you can edit the size, feather, and angle of your brush.

The fade function is a great addition to brushes in Elements. You can use this option to change the

fade-out point of a brush stroke, similar to when making a stroke with a paintbrush — it begins dark and full, and as the paint runs out, the stroke fades away. Other options include spacing, which allows you to create dotted lines instead of solid lines, and color jitter, which affects the color and placement of your brush dots. When you create a custom brush, the selected options stay active for the next time you use the brush.

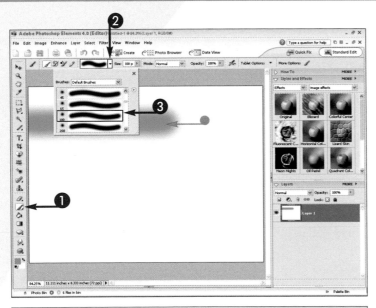

① Click the Brush tool.

② Click here to display the Brushes palette.

③ Select a brush.

● The image shows a straight line drawn with the brush you selected.

④ Click the More Options button to open the Brush Options dialog box.

⑤ Click and drag the sliders to adjust the values.

⑥ Adjust here (or enter values) to alter the angle and roundness of the brush tip.

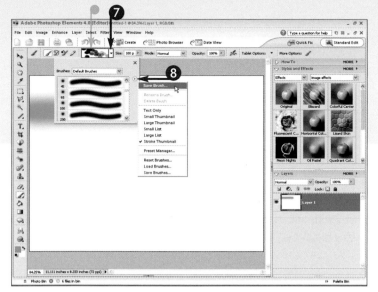

- The Brush example reflects the new settings.

7 Click here to display the Brushes palette.

8 Click here and select Save Brush.

 # 26

DIFFICULTY LEVEL

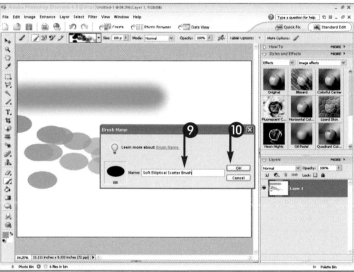

The Brush Name dialog box appears.

9 Type a name for the brush.

10 Click OK.

The custom brush appears in the menu.

The image shows a straight line drawn with the custom brush.

TIPS

Customize It!

You can create highly detailed custom brushes from photographic images. Using any selection tool, make a selection in your image, then click Edit, and then click Define Brush Using Selection. The Brush Name dialog box appears. Type a name for your new brush and then click OK. Your new brush appears in the Brush drop-down menu.

Did You Know?

You can draw straight lines using your brush by clicking in the image where you want your line to begin, releasing the mouse, moving the cursor to where you want the line to end, and then pressing Shift+click at your destination point. A straight line appears between the two points, using the current brush selection.

Work with
SHAPES

You can use the Shape tools to create a variety of geometric shapes from the Elements library of shapes. The Custom Shape library contains many different shapes, from animals to fancy ornaments. You can select a shape from the menu, and then click and drag your cursor to the size and dimensions of the shape you want.

You can now use six different Shape tools in Elements 4: Rectangle, Rounded Rectangle, Ellipse, Polygon, Line, and the Custom Shape tool. Although

the first four tools are basic geometric shapes, the Polygon Shape tool allows you to create straight edge shapes with a custom number of sides. The Custom Shape tool has specialty shapes for other uses. See Task #29 for more information about custom shapes.

The Shape tools lets you quickly make geometric shapes that may otherwise be difficult to reproduce manually. For example, although you can create a hexagonal shape manually, it would take a while to create six equilateral lines at the same correct angles.

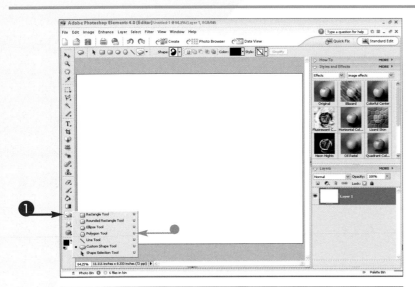

① Click and hold the mouse cursor over the Custom Shape tool.

● The Shape tool menu appears.

② Click a tool.

③ Click here and select or type a shape option, if applicable.

Note: Some Elements shapes have additional options on the Options bar.

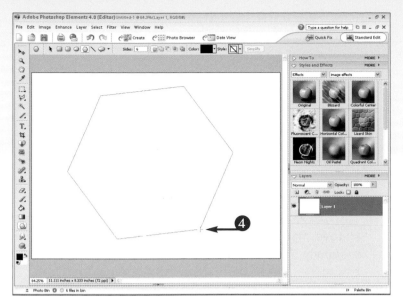

27

④ Click and drag the tool to create the shape you want.

Elements draws the shape from the point of origin outward in all directions.

Press and hold the Shift key while dragging to constrain shapes to equal proportions, such as squares and perfect circles.

DIFFICULTY LEVEL

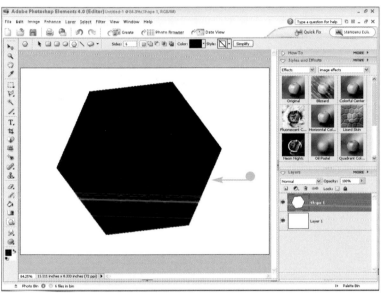

● Your shape appears on-screen.

TIPS

Customize It!

Your shape appears in the same color that you have selected as your foreground color. If you decide that this color is not for you, click the Color box in the Options bar and select a new color from the Color Picker that appears. You can also set your foreground color before drawing with the Shape tool.

Did You Know?

Several of the geometric shapes offer additional options in the Options bar. For example, when you click the Rounded Rectangle Shape tool, you can set the radius of the rounded corners. The Polygon Shape tool allows you to specify the number of sides for your polygon, from 3-sided to 100-sided.

Add
SHAPE STYLES

You can use layer styles to enhance the appearance of your shapes. The Layer Styles palette offers different style categories that can produce a wide range of results. You can apply these styles to any shape design that you create, including bevels, shadows, and glows, which can add depth and pizzazz to your graphics.

Elements also enables you to add complex layer styles, which generates more interesting and complex effects to your shapes, such as chrome, glass, and even cactus patterns. These styles give character to

the shapes, even more so than basic bevels and shadows. You can create dynamic graphics from the large library of complex layer styles.

After you apply a style, you can click the *f* icon 🔎 in the shape layer and adjust the components of the applied layer style. For example, you can adjust the scale of your styles to fit different-sized shapes, alter the distance of the shadows, or even increase the depth of a bevel. Each style can affect different attributes, so experiment to see the results you can create.

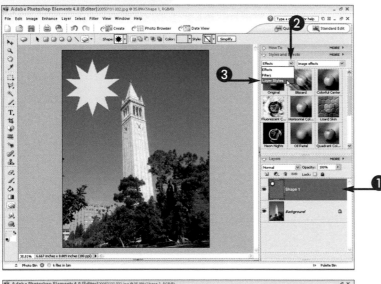

① Click the Shape layer.

② Click here to open the Styles and Effects palette.

③ Click Layer Styles.

● The Layer Styles palette appears.

④ Click here and select a layer style category.

28

DIFFICULTY LEVEL

● Elements applies the layer style to your shape.

Customize It!

You can transform your shapes to add perspective and to resize the shapes to fit your needs. Click the layer that contains the shape, and then click Image, Transform, and then a transform command. Drag the bounding box handles to scale and transform your shape.

Did You Know?

You can add shape styles at the same time that you draw your shape. The Shape tool Options bar contains a drop-down menu marked Style. Click the menu to open the Layer Styles palette. Select the category and style design you want in order to customize your shape at the time you are drawing.

Design with
CUSTOM SHAPES

You can use the Shape tool to generate different geometric shapes for a variety of purposes and projects. The Custom Shapes palette offers you access to a wide variety of new and unusual shapes, such as animals and fancy ornaments. You can choose from 16 different categories within the shape library of Elements 4, each of which has it own unique set of designs. This library of more than 500

custom shapes opens the door to more creative designs, such as logos and Web page buttons.

Like regular geometrical shapes, custom shapes are vector graphics that can accept dozens of layer styles that enhance their appearance. Like all shapes, custom shapes become simplified and pixel-based when you apply filters or effects to them.

❶ Click the Custom Shape tool.

❷ Click here to open the Shape palette.

The Shape palette appears.

❸ Click the shape you want.

● You can change the color of your custom shape by clicking here.

4 Click and drag to draw your custom shape.

5 Release the mouse button.

6 Repeat steps **1** to **5** to add more custom shapes.

DIFFICULTY LEVEL

● The custom shape appears.

This example shows some additional layers that were added.

Caution!
Because vector graphics are so versatile for resizing and editing, it is strongly recommended that if you need to apply a filter, shape, or other simplifying action, that you apply the filter on a duplicate layer. After you simplify a vector graphic, it becomes a pixel-based graphic and loses some of its versatility for editing.

Did You Know?
You can use custom shapes as masks for other graphics. Place a texture or image above a shape layer. Click Layer and then Group with Previous. The shape acts like a mask, only revealing your image in the outline of the custom shape. The new Cookie Cutter tool can use any custom shape to create a cutout of your image.

Import additional
BRUSHES AND SHAPES

You can import brushes and shapes from outside of Photoshop Elements for use inside the program. Many websites offer different custom brushes and shapes, and this is a great way to obtain new designs and graphics. In addition, you can use brushes and shapes designed for Adobe Photoshop in Photoshop Elements 3 as well.

You can import these custom sets by copying their files into the appropriate directory. When you start Elements, the program automatically loads the brushes, shapes, and other presets found within the default folders.

Brush files have the .abr extension, and Shape files have the .csh extension. You can identify the correct folders by the files within. By default, you can find both Brushes and Custom Shapes folders at C:\Program Files\Adobe\Photoshop Elements 3\Presets. After you load them, you can click the Shape selection options menu to load a new set, or you can click Load Brushes in the Brush selection menu options.

You can find incredible brushes and shapes at many different locations online. For more information about online resources, see Chapter 7.

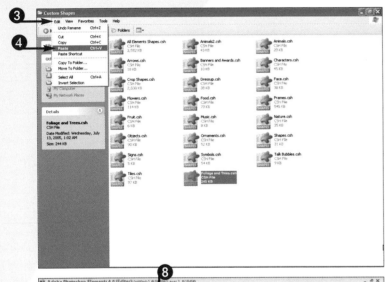

① Copy the CSH shape file from an online or external location to your computer.

② In Windows Explorer, go to C:\Program Files\Adobe\ Photoshop Elements 4.0\ Presets\Custom Shapes.

③ Click Edit.

④ Click paste from the drop-down menu to paste the CSH file into the folder.

You can also press Ctrl+V to paste the CSH file into the folder.

⑤ Restart Elements.

⑥ Click here to open a new document.

⑦ Click the Custom Shape tool.

⑧ Click here to display the Custom Shapes palette.

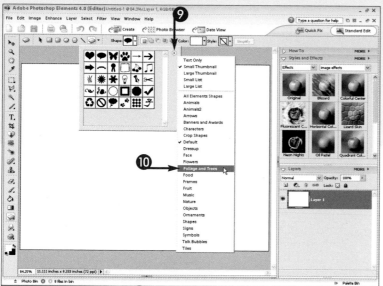

⑨ Click here to open the Custom Shapes palette drop-down list.

⑩ Click the new shape set.

DIFFICULTY LEVEL

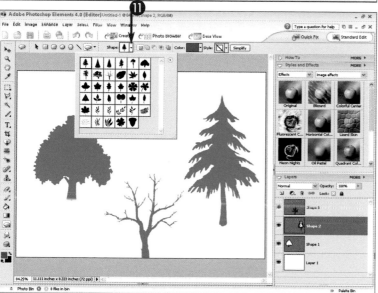

⑪ Click here to view the new shape selections.

TIPS

Did You Know?

You can easily install your imported brushes. Paste your ABR file in the Preset/Brushes folder. Restart Elements, and in the Brush selection menu options, click Load Brushes. In the Open dialog box that appears, open the brush file you want by clicking the file, and then click OK. You can now use your new brush set by clicking the Brush selection drop-down menu.

Did You Know?

You can always return to your original brush and shape sets. The Brush selection drop-down menu contains an option to Reset Brushes. The Shape selection drop-down menu also contains a Default shapes setting. Clicking either of these two choices resets the corresponding tool's default sets.

Chapter

4

Working with Photos

Photoshop Elements includes a variety of features that are designed specifically for fixing or enhancing digital photographs.

One of the most common uses of Photoshop Elements is to correct and optimize photographs that have been shot with a digital camera. This chapter introduces you to a versatile interface that allows you to do this — the Quick Fix dialog box. This dialog box gives you easy access to tools that enable you to apply exposure, color-correction, and other tools to fix digital photos.

Scanned photographs offer another set of challenges, and this chapter features tips that enable you to tackle them as well. You can also use the Healing Brush tool to remove

dust, scratches, and other artifacts that may be introduced during the scanning process.

Some tasks in this chapter show you how to use Photoshop Elements to combine separate photographs into a final composition. For example, you can use the Photomerge feature to stitch several images together into a single panoramic image. When you use the Photomerge feature, you identify your source photos, and then Photoshop Elements attempts to create the panorama for you automatically. You can also arrange several photos on a single canvas to create a digital montage. Photoshop Elements makes it easy to create a montage by organizing the pasted images into separate layers.

Top 100

Apply a
QUICK FIX
to a photo

You can apply exposure, color-correction, and other enhancement tools to your images using the Quick Fix dialog box. All of the tools in this dialog box are accessible through other Photoshop Elements commands. The Quick Fix dialog box simply gathers the tools under one convenient, easy-to-use interface. As you apply the Quick Fix tools, you can compare an original version of your photo with a version to which you have applied enhancements.

The Lighting tools available in the dialog box give you several ways to fix photos that have been under- or overexposed. For example, the Contrast and Levels tools offer simple, one-click adjustments for bad lighting, or you can use the Contrast sliders for custom fine-tuning of shadows, midtones, and highlights, to correct specific problem areas in a photo.

The Quick Fix dialog box also features Focus tools for photos that are blurry, and Rotate tools for photos that need to be flipped or rotated. There is also a Smart Fix Auto button that applies optimized settings to the image.

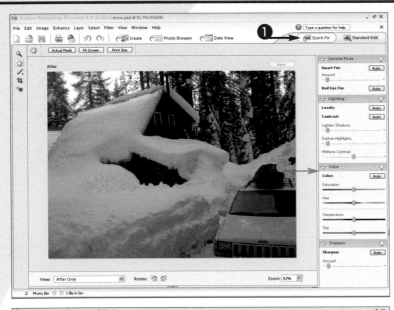

1. Click Quick Fix.

● The Quick Fix dialog box appears.

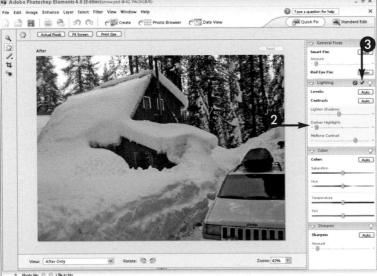

2. Click and drag a slider to adjust settings.

   This example adjusts the lighting to improve the tone.

3. Click the Commit button to apply the adjustment.

   Note: Making an adjustment in a different category automatically applies the last changes you made.

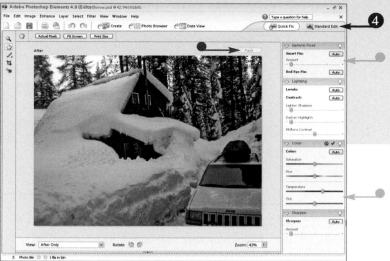

- You can continue to make adjustments in other categories.

  This example boosts the saturation and temperature to enrich the colors in the photo.

- You can click the Reset button to revert to the saved image, shown on the left.

④ Click the Standard Edit tab.

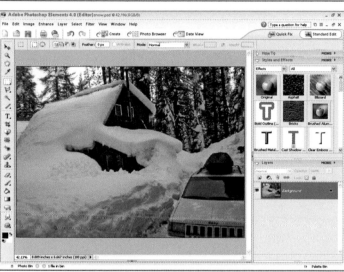

Elements applies the Quick Fix adjustments to the image.

Elements returns to Standard Edit screen.

TIPS

Did You Know?

There are several ways to undo the changes that you apply in the Quick Fix dialog box. For example, you can click the Undo button (⟲) to undo the most recent Quick Fix adjustments. You can also redo an adjustment that was just undone by clicking the Redo button(⟳). Clicking the Reset button (Reset) reverts the image to the state that it was in when you opened the Quick Fix dialog box.

Customize It!

While in Quick Fix mode, you can save and open files normally, as well as use most menu options. However, you cannot access the standard toolbar in Quick Fix mode. To access the standard toolbar and remaining menu options, return to Standard Edit mode.

Repair photos with the
HEALING BRUSH TOOL

Although many older photographs contain smudges, artifacts, or dust, these imperfections do not usually affect our enjoyment of these images. Occasionally, more serious problems, such as a burr on the film that cuts across a crucial area of the image, require some attention.

With Photoshop Elements, you can use several tools to correct this problem. However, with some of these tools, the final result may appear artificial, or "off" and will not look the same as the area surrounding the correction.

Photoshop Elements offers the Healing Brush tool to make this type of correction easier. All of the cloning tools, including the Healing Brush, use a sampled area of an image to apply a correction to the target area. The key difference with the Healing Brush tool is that it not only brushes the target area with the sampled source area, but it also matches the texture, lighting, and shading of the sampled pixels to those of the target pixels. As a result, this brush creates a smoother and more seamless correction.

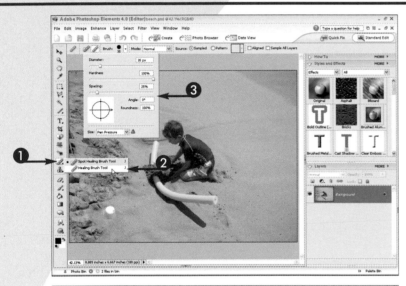

1 Click the Spot Healing Brush tool.

2 In the pop-up menu, click Healing Brush Tool.

3 Click the options you want.

4 Click a source area while pressing and holding the Alt key.

The cursor changes to a cross pointer (⊕).

⑤ Apply the brush to the area that you want to correct.

The source point moves in alignment with the brush tip.

The Healing Brush tool repairs the area with source pixels.

The Healing Brush tool corrects the flaw.

This example shows the final results following several applications of the Healing Brush tool.

Customize It!

By using selected areas close to the flaw you are trying to correct, you can obtain texture, lighting, and shading that are more consistent with the surrounding area.

Did You Know?

You can avoid duplicating work by making smaller, more frequent brush strokes. When you make a correction with a large stroke, and use the Undo command, you must redo all the work up to the error for that stroke. It is better to use smaller strokes, and to sample often. This way, if you use the Undo command, there is less make-up work necessary to return to your point of error. Although more time-consuming, this method produces better results.

Make quick repairs with the
SPOT HEALING BRUSH TOOL

You can use the powerful brushes in Photoshop Elements to quickly remove dust and blemishes that can ruin or detract from an otherwise excellent photo. The Spot Healing Brush tool allows you to select from many brush shapes and designs. You can then remove imperfections from a photograph by adjusting the selected pixels with the surrounding pixels.

The main difference between the Spot Healing Brush tool and the Healing Brush tool is that the Spot Healing Brush tool applies your changes by using surrounding pixels from around the brush shape, as opposed to pixels from a selected area.

The Spot Healing Brush tool has two brush types, Proximity Match and Create Texture. With Proximity Match, the Spot Healing Brush takes a mixture of brush-sized and -shaped selections around the covered area and blends them together. The Create Texture type takes the brushed area and applies its changes by matching the texture, lighting, and shading of the surrounding pixels to those of the target pixels. Similar to the Healing Brush, this creates a more smooth and seamless repair.

❶ Click the Spot Healing Brush tool.

❷ Select a brush blending type.

This example uses the Create Texture type.

❸ Click here and select a brush shape and size.

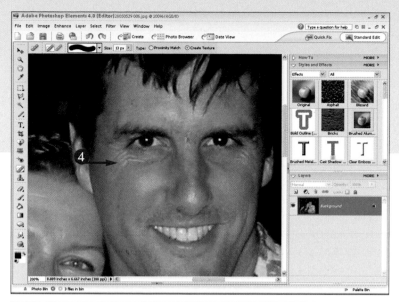

④ Click and drag over the area you want to change.

A marquee appears, indicating your selection.

⑤ Release the mouse button.

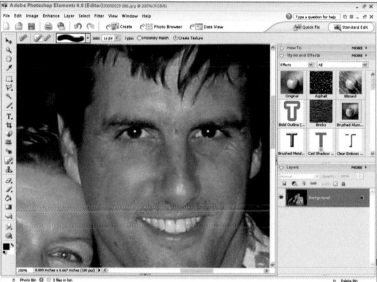

The Spot Healing Brush tool repairs the area you selected, using the surrounding pixels.

Did You Know?
The type of brush that you select can affect your results. For example, feathered or soft-edged brushes create a different blend of pixels than hard-edged brushes. You can also experiment with different brush shapes to obtain different results.

Put It Together!
You can easily switch back and forth between the Spot Healing Brush tool and the Healing Brush tool. As with many related tools, the Options bar at the top of the screen has buttons that switch you from one tool to the other, without having to access the pop-up menu. This allows you to do large-scale corrections with the Healing Brush tool and to fine-tune with the Spot Healing Brush tool, using a single mouse click.

Create a
PANORAMIC PHOTO
to show more detail

You can use the Photomerge feature in Photoshop Elements to merge several images together into a single panoramic image. Panoramic images are usually much wider than they are tall. As a result, they enable you to display more scenery in a single image than is usually possible in a normal photograph.

When you set up a Photomerge composition, you identify your source photos. Then Photoshop Elements attempts to create the panorama for you automatically by aligning similar overlapping pixel patterns along the edges. After the panorama is complete, you can still make changes to the placement of the individual source photos. This enables you to correct alignment problems that may occur during the merging process.

The Photomerge dialog box helps you to create the panoramic compositions. The dialog box includes tools for manipulating the source photos, a lightbox for organizing source images that are not in use, and a work area for assembling the panorama. There are also settings for adjusting perspective in the completed image.

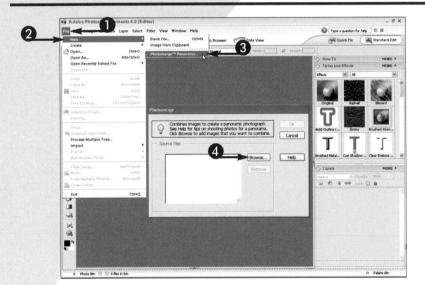

① Click File.

② Click New.

③ Click Photomerge™ Panorama.

The Photomerge dialog box appears.

④ Click Browse.

The Open dialog box appears.

⑤ Click here and select the folder that contains the source images you want to merge.

⑥ Press Shift and then click the images you want to merge.

⑦ Click Open.

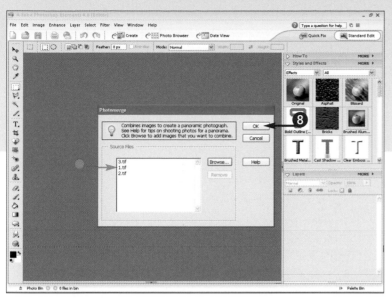

● The filenames of the images appear in the Source Files list.

⑧ Click OK.

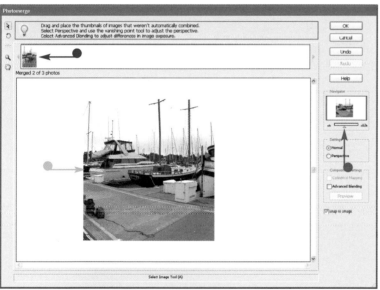

● Elements attempts to merge the images together into a single panoramic image.

● Thumbnails of the images that it cannot merge appear in the lightbox area.

● You can click and drag the slider to zoom the panoramic image in and out.

TIPS

Did You Know?

A wide-angle lens can help you to maximize the field of view in your source photographs as well as in your resulting panorama. However, you should avoid fisheye lenses when creating panoramas, because they can distort your photographs and make it harder for the Photoshop Elements software to combine your images.

Did You Know?

Consistent exposure throughout your set of source photos is key to creating attractive panoramas. For example, using a flash in some of the photos but not in others can make blending them together difficult; it can also result in a panorama in which the lighting shifts unnaturally across the picture.

Create a
PANORAMIC PHOTO
to show more detail

When you create a panoramic image, you may need to reposition an individual source file, or rotate a file in your composition in order to achieve consistent blending. The editing tools in the Photomerge dialog box help you to perform these tasks with relative ease. You can also zoom in and out to more closely check the alignment of each file.

You can save time and also avoid having to make manual adjustments by using source photos that have the right amount of overlap. For the best

results, your source photos should overlap one another by approximately 15% to 40%. If the overlap is less than 15%, then Photomerge may not be able to automatically assemble the panorama.

After your panorama is complete, you can edit and make adjustments to it just like any other Photoshop Elements image. For example, you can make exposure adjustments to the seams where the source photos were combined.

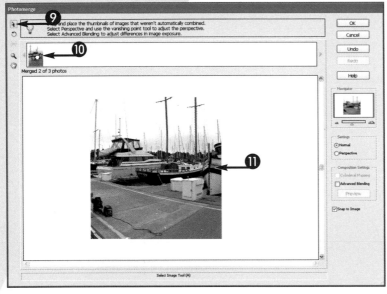

9 Click the Select Image tool.

10 Click and drag an image from the lightbox area to the work area.

11 Position the image so that it lines up with the neighboring image in the panorama.

● If you select Snap to Image (☐ changes to ☑), Elements tries to align the image edges after you click and drag the new image into the work area.

● You can use the Hand tool to adjust the entire panoramic image inside the main window.

12 Repeat steps **10** and **11** for other images in the lightbox area so that they overlap and match one another.

● To align image seams that are not level with one another, you can click the Rotate Image tool and click and drag on the image sections in the work area.

⓭ Click OK.

● You can click Undo or press Ctrl+Z to undo your Photomerge commands one at a time.

Elements merges the images and opens the resulting panorama in a new image window.

● You can use the Crop tool to remove any blank space on the sides of the image.

Did You Know?

The more level that your photographs are relative to one another, the easier they should be to merge into a single panorama. Using a tripod when shooting your photos can help to make them as level as possible.

Did You Know?

While most of your panoramas may consist of horizontal arrangements of photos, you can also use Photoshop Elements to create vertical panoramas. To create a vertical panorama, first rotate your source photos by 90 degrees. This allows you to merge them together as if they were a horizontal panorama. Rotate the resulting panorama by 90 degrees in the opposite direction to obtain your vertical panorama.

Separate multiple images with
AUTO DIVIDE

You can import images directly into Photoshop Elements using your scanner. Most scanners can scan multiple photos, which Elements then imports as a single image. The task of placing the individual photos into their own documents using selection tools and copy commands can be time consuming and tedious. Elements now has a new automation tool called Auto Divide that can perform this task for you quickly and effectively, separating your scanned image into individual documents.

With the scanned image file open, you can crop and straighten the photos. Elements automatically

searches the scanned image for the right-angled corners of individual photos, selects a photo, rotates, copies, and pastes it into a new document, and then returns to the original scan for the next photo. One benefit is that the individual images are copies, so you can save the original scan for future use.

For bulk-scanning projects, the new Crop and Straighten Photos command is an invaluable time-saving feature. For example, you can use it to scan images for projects such as family photo albums and yearbook pages.

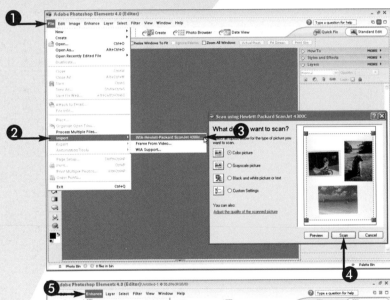

① Click File.

② Click Import.

A list of available input sources appears.

③ Click a scanner in the drop-down menu.

Elements uses your scanner software to import the images.

④ Click the button that begins the scanning process.

● Elements imports the scanned image that contains all of the photos.

⑤ To make adjustments to the image, click Enhance and select a menu option.

This example applies the Auto Levels command.

6 Click Image.

7 Click Divide Scanned Photos.

35

Elements crops and straightens the photos and extracts the individual images into separate documents.

During this process, Elements also trims the excess whitespace from the outside edges of each extracted image.

Customize It!

You can make the Auto Divide feature work more efficiently by properly arranging your images on the scanner. Placing images too close together can cause Elements to save the images to the same file, because it may not recognize that the images are separate. Space your photos apart, especially if they do not have clearly defined edges. You should also place the photos as straight as possible on the scanner. Elements does not always rotate an image to align with a perfectly horizontal or vertical angle. If the image is still slightly off, you can rotate it in the new document by clicking Image, clicking Rotate Canvas, and then clicking Arbitrary.

REMOVE UNWANTED OBJECTS
in a photo

You can use the Clone Stamp tool on your photographs to remove scratches, dust specks, and other objects that you do not want in your scenes. To remove unwanted objects from your photo, you can copy a different area of your photo, where objects are not present, and paste over the unwanted objects. If the copied area is similar enough to the background around the unwanted objects, the results can be seamless — no one should know the objects were ever there.

You should first constrain the area around the unwanted objects with a selection tool before applying the Clone Stamp. This method ensures that the Clone Stamp tool does not affect the scenery near the unwanted objects. You may find that the Lasso tool is easier to use when selecting objects with curved or soft edges.

You can also use a combination of different textures and backgrounds in the scene to cover up the unwanted objects. This technique can make it less obvious that objects were removed.

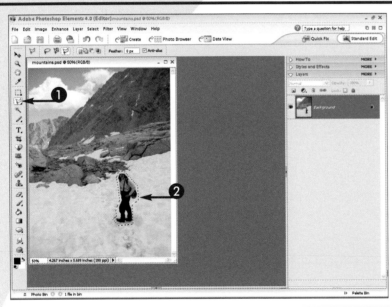

① Click a selection tool.

② Draw a selection border around the unwanted object.

It is important to leave extra space between the edges of the object and the background.

③ Click the Clone Stamp tool.

④ Press and hold Alt.

● The cursor changes to a cross pointer ($\oplus$).

⑤ Click the background area that you want to copy over the unwanted object.

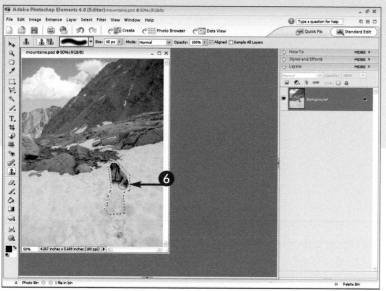

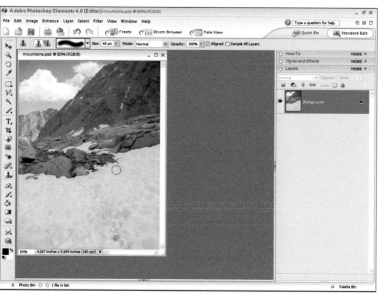

6 Click and drag inside the selection to copy the background over the unwanted object.

7 If necessary, repeat steps **5** and **6** until the unwanted object is covered up.

DIFFICULTY LEVEL

8 Press Ctrl+D to deselect the selection.

The unwanted object is removed.

TIPS

Customize It!

When erasing unwanted objects, your photo should have appropriate scenery, with consistent color and lighting. However, if this is not the case, you should still be able to make the changes you want. For example, if the only scenery available is of a slightly different color or shading, you can use the opacity setting of the Clone Stamp tool. By adjusting the setting to less than 100 percent and using small strokes or dabs, you can clone semitransparent copies of different areas of the scenery to make up for areas that do not exactly match.

Customize It!

You can change the size of the Clone Stamp tool by using the menu on the Options bar or by typing the opening and closing brackets ([ ]).

REMOVE RED-EYE
from photos

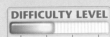

Red-eye is the eerie effect that occurs when the camera flash reflects off the inside of a subject's eye, or retina. Red-eye often occurs when you take flash photos in darkness or very low light. You can quickly and easily remove red-eye from a photo using the Red Eye Removal tool.

When you place the crosshairs over the affected eye and click the mouse, Elements samples the reddish pixels in the area and adjusts them, based on a predefined darkness value. The Red Eye Removal tool changes the hue of the affected eye, without

changing the brightness. This allows the Red Eye Removal tool to remove the redness without getting rid of lightness or contrast.

An important setting for the Red Eye Removal tool is the Relative Pupil Size. This setting specifies the size and tolerance of the affected area. A low tolerance setting may not remove all of the red in the eye, while a high setting may overly darken the eye, making it look even stranger than before.

DIFFICULTY LEVEL

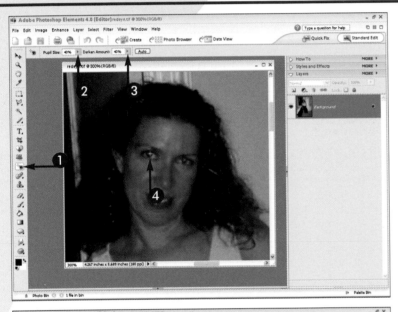

① Click the Red Eye Removal tool.

② Click here and select the relative size of the pupil.

③ Click here and select the pupil darkness.

④ Click the red-eye of the subject.

● Elements replaces the red pixels using the settings that you selected.

SCALE AN IMAGE
to change its size

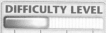

You can scale an image to change its relative size. This can be useful to fit an image in with other elements on a Web page, or if you want to fit your image to a common photo size.

Resizing for the Web involves increasing or decreasing the pixel dimensions of an image. The size at which an image prints, or the document size, depends on the number of pixels as well as the print resolution. When you change the document size in the Image Size dialog box, Elements adjusts the image so that it prints at the specified dimensions.

DIFFICULTY LEVEL

Customize It!

You can change your image resolution in the Image Size dialog box. Changing the resolution does not affect the number of pixels in the screen or Web page size of the image. However, it does affect how the image prints out. Increasing the resolution shrinks the image on the page; decreasing the resolution enlarges it.

① Click Image.
② Click Resize.
③ Click Image Size.

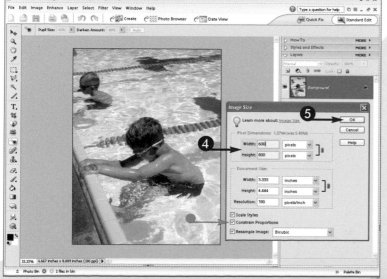

The Image Size dialog box appears.

④ Type a new size for the image.

● You can click Constrain Proportions (☐ changes to ☑) to scale proportionally.

⑤ Click OK.

The image is resized to the new dimensions.

Give photographs a sepia tone with the
PHOTO FILTER

You can create professional effects with the new Photo Filter command. Elements uses adjustment layers to apply a color overlay to the image, similar to the color filters that professional photographers use. You can select from 20 different preset photo filters.

Although a photographer must use an actual filter over the lens during the exposure of the photo, you can apply the photo filters to images after the photo is taken. The names of many of the photo filters match those of standard lens filters that have been used by photographers for years. Many of the filters

were designed to change the characteristics of light when exposing the film. Adobe offers descriptions of these filters in their online user's guide, but you can find more information online at www.tiffen.com and www.hoyaoptics.com.

You can apply the Photo Filter command to a full image or to an individual layer or object. If you want to apply a Photo Filter command to an entire image that contains layers, then you must first merge the layers, or apply separate Photo Filter commands to each layer.

① Click Filter.
② Click Adjustments.
③ Click Photo Filter.

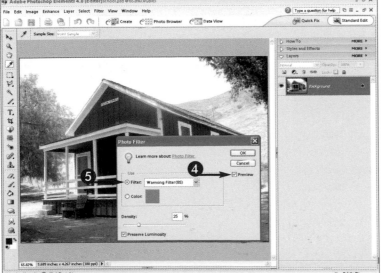

The Photo Filter dialog box appears.

④ Click the Preview check box to preview the effect (☐ changes to ☑).

⑤ Click the Filter radio button to activate the Filter drop-down menu (○ changes to ⊙).

6 Click the drop-down arrow.

7 Select a photo filter style.

8 Click and drag the slider to adjust the density of the filter.

9 Click OK.

DIFFICULTY LEVEL

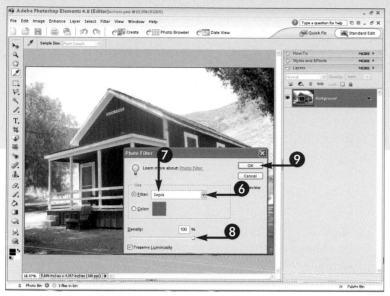

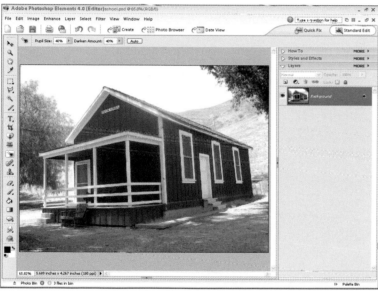

Elements applies the photo filter.

Customize It!

Sepia is just one of the many color filters that you can apply to your photo. You can also select custom colors by clicking the Color Picker box in the Photo Filter dialog box.

Did You Know?

Unlike adjustment layers, the Photo Filter adjustments affect the image directly. After you apply the Photo Filter command, your image is permanently changed, unless you use the Undo command. You should test the filter on a copy of the image or layer prior to applying the filter.

Did You Know?

If you want to remove all traces of color from a photo before applying the sepia tone, you can click Enhance, Adjust Color, and then Remove Color.

CROP PHOTOS
to remove clutter

You can improve a photo by using the Crop tool to trim areas from the photo. For example, trimming areas from the sides of a photo can change the relative prominence of particular objects in the photo. Cropping can also remove unnecessary image content and thereby reduce the file size of the final image. This can be important if you are using the image on a website, where a smaller file size results in faster downloading.

You can also use the Crop tool to add extra space around your image to give it a distinctive framed appearance. To add extra space, you must first increase the area of the image window so that the Crop tool can extend beyond the boundaries of the image. Dragging the Crop tool outside the boundary and then applying the crop in this manner increases the canvas size.

Keep in mind that cropping an image affects all of the layers in the image, including layers that are currently not selected or visible.

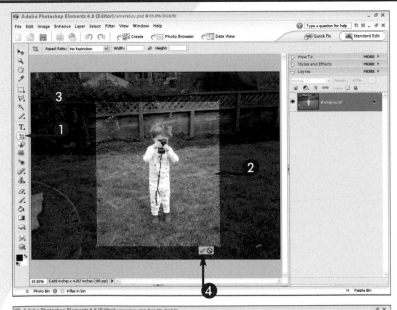

TRIM AND CROP A PHOTO

1 Click the Crop tool.

2 Click and drag inside the photo to define the cropping boundary.

3 Click and drag the crop handles to fine-tune the cropping boundary.

4 Click the Commit button to apply the change.

Elements crops the photo.

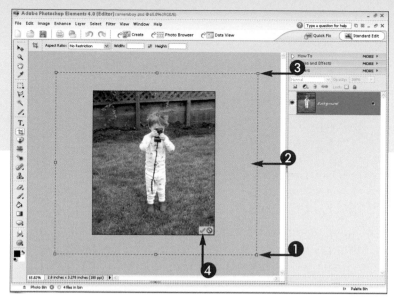

#40

DIFFICULTY LEVEL

① Click and drag the corner of the image window to add extra space around the photo.

② Click and drag the Crop tool to define the cropping area.

③ Click and drag the handles to extend the cropping area outside the boundary of the photo.

④ Click the Commit button to apply the change.

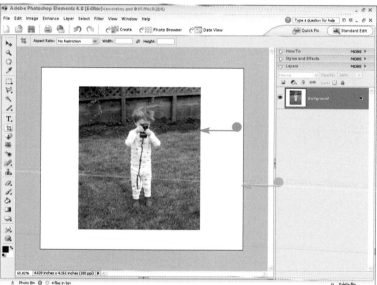

● Elements crops the photo.

● Elements adds extra space to the edges of the cropped area, using the current background color.

TIPS

Did You Know?

You can crop a photo using any selection tool. First, use a selection tool to select the area you want to crop. Click Image and then click Crop. Elements crops the image to the outermost width and height dimensions of your selection.

Customize It!

When you select the Crop tool (⌗), you can use the dialog boxes in the Options bar to specify the dimensions and resolution of the resulting image. Enter values in the Height, Width, and Resolution boxes. You can automatically add the dimensions and resolution of the current image by clicking the Front Image icon in the Options bar.

Chapter 5

Working with Color, Print, and the Web

Accurate, vibrant color is crucial to any successful digital photography project, whether for print or the Web. Photoshop Elements offers many features that enable you to adjust and optimize color, including the Color Variations, Color Cast, and Replace Color tools. The Color Variations tool offers a powerful but user-friendly way to adjust the overall color balance of your digital images. With a single mouse click, the Color Cast tool gives you the ability to remove unnatural tints that can create a color cast in your image. The Replace Color tool allows you to quickly and easily select all of the instances of a given color, and then replace it with a different hue or change its brightness or intensity.

The Print feature in Elements allows you to preview a printout of your image, and gives you interactive tools with which you can fine-tune the orientation and final image before it is printed. For more printing options, see Chapter 9, which describes additional print and Web features that are available in the Organizer section of Elements 4.

The Save for Web dialog box is a powerful feature that allows you to save your files in the two most popular formats for Web images, GIF and JPEG. You can specify several options for both image types, including quality and size. You can even create an animated GIF to make your Web projects more interesting and fun.

Top 100

Adjust the
COLOR VARIATIONS
of an image

You can adjust the color balance, contrast, and saturation of an image using the Color Variations dialog box. As you make successive adjustments to your image, you can compare its current state with the state of the image when you opened the dialog box. When you are satisfied with your changes and click the OK button, Elements applies your adjustments to the image.

You can use the Color Variations feature to adjust the color or exposure of a flawed image that was shot

with a digital camera or digitized with a scanner. You can also use it to match up the appearance of two different photos so that they both have similar color content and overall lighting.

The settings in the dialog box allow you to affect a specific range of colors in your image, for example, only the colors in the darkest or lightest parts of the image. They also enable you to adjust the degree of change, so you can intensify or lighten the amount of change you apply.

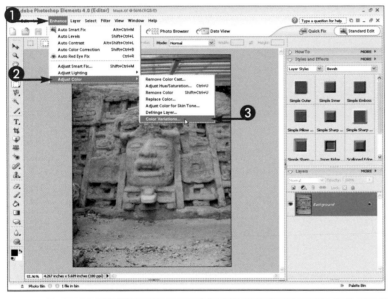

① Click Enhance.

② Click Adjust Color.

③ Click Color Variations.

The Color Variations dialog box appears.

④ Click a tonal range to which you want to apply your effects (○ changes to ◉).

● Alternatively, you can click Saturation, which indicates strength of color (○ changes to ◉).

⑤ Click and drag the Amount slider left to make small adjustments, or right to make large adjustments.

⑥ To change the color in your image, click one of the thumbnails.

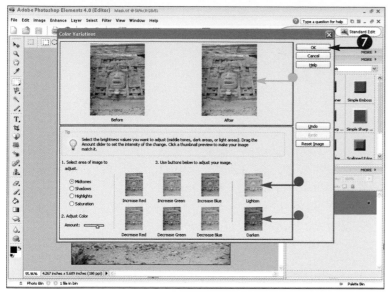

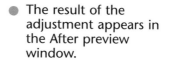

● The result of the adjustment appears in the After preview window.

To further adjust the effect, you can click one of the thumbnails again.

● You can increase the brightness of the image by clicking Lighten.

● You can decrease the brightness by clicking Darken.

7 Click OK.

Elements applies your color adjustments to the image.

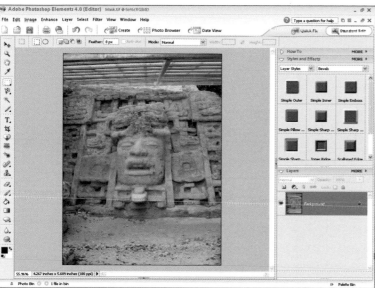

Did You Know?

While the Color Variations dialog box is open, there are several ways to undo the changes that you apply. You can click the Undo button to undo the most recent Variations adjustment. You can also click an Increase or Decrease button to undo a previous Decrease or Increase command. You can click Reset Image to revert the image to its original state before you open the dialog box.

Did You Know?

The Color Variations dialog box is just one way in which you can remove a color cast, such as the yellowish tint that often appears in old photographic prints. Another way to remove a color cast is with the Color Cast command, which is described in Task #43.

Paint a
BLACK-AND-WHITE
photo

You can apply color to a black-and-white photo using the Brush tool. This is a great way to draw attention to interesting objects in an otherwise colorless scene. When you apply the Brush tool, it adds the current foreground color to your image.

You can customize your brush to meet your needs. A menu on the Options bar offers a selection of preset Brush sizes with either hard or soft edges. You should choose a brush size that is compatible with the size of the objects you want to paint; you can place the Brush cursor over the object to help you

decide. Brushes with hard edges are useful for well-defined objects; soft edges can give you flexibility when painting objects with fuzzy silhouettes.

You can also customize your Brush tool by changing its blending mode. The blending mode determines how the color that you add with the brush blends with the existing colors in your image. For example, in Normal mode, the Brush tool applies an opaque layer of color to your image, which covers up existing details. To maintain the details in your image, you can select Color mode instead.

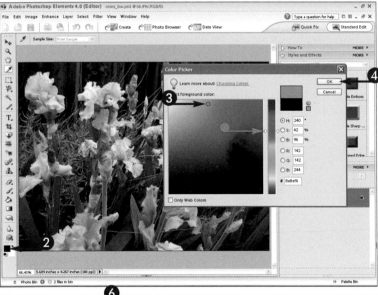

① Open a black-and-white image.

Note: The image must be in RGB mode if you want to add color. See Task #44 for more information.

② Click the Foreground Color box.

The Color Picker appears.

③ Click in the color box spectrum to select a paint color.

● You can click and drag the slider to change the selection of colors.

④ Click OK.

The foreground color changes to the new color.

⑤ Click the Brush tool.

⑥ Click here and select a brush style.

⑦ Press Enter.

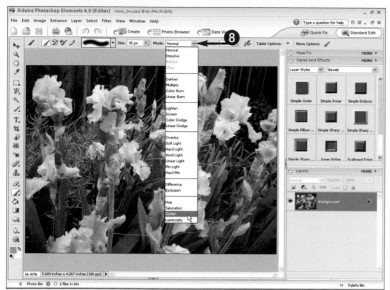

8 Click here and select Color.

When you paint in Color mode, you apply color without losing image detail.

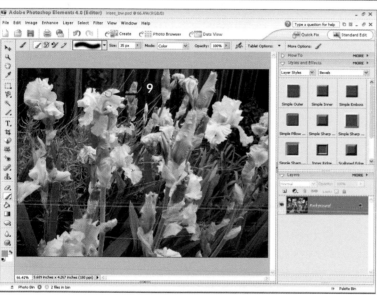

9 Click and drag inside the image to apply the color.

The Brush tool adds color to the image.

TIPS

Did You Know?

To protect areas in your image that you want to leave black and white, you can make a selection using any selection tool before you start painting. Elements only allows you to paint the area inside your selection.

Did You Know?

You can use the Paint Bucket tool to quickly color all of the pixels inside a selection. The Paint Bucket tool applies color to the area where you click, along with any surrounding pixels of a similar color.

Customize It!

You can decrease the amount of color that you add with your Paint Brush tool by decreasing its opacity to less than 100 percent in the Options bar. This is useful if you want to apply a semitransparent layer of color.

Remove a COLOR CAST

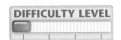

You can use the Color Cast command to remove an unwanted tint from a digital photograph. Removing a color cast results in a more pleasing image by revealing the original color balance of a photo.

A color cast can result from a variety of factors. For example, an outdoor scene under clear skies may contain a naturally occurring blue cast; an indoor scene may have a cast due to light coming through tinted windows; if you are working with a scanned photo image, the cast may be the result of a poorly developed print or an uncalibrated scanner.

The Color Cast command is easy to apply. You must first click the Color Cast eyedropper on an area of the photo that should be neutral in color, for example, white, gray, or black. Elements adjusts the overall color, based on the tint of the pixel you select. You may have to click several different places in your image to find a result that is acceptable.

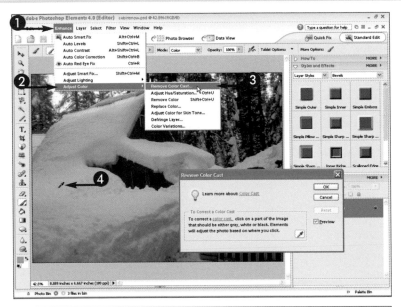

① Click Enhance.

② Click Adjust Color.

③ Click Remove Color Cast.

The Remove Color Cast dialog box appears.

④ Click a part of your image that is affected by the color cast.

Elements removes the color cast from the image.

● You can click Reset to revert to the original color cast and try again.

⑤ Click OK.

Elements applies the correction.

CHANGE THE MODE
of an image

You can switch between several different image modes in Elements. For example, you may want to change the mode to increase the number of available colors or to reduce the file size of your image. The modes that are available in Elements include RGB Color, Bitmap, Grayscale, and Indexed Color.

RGB Color is the most commonly used mode, as it has the fewest restrictions, and allows you to work with all types of colors. In addition, some Elements commands only work in RGB Color mode.

Bitmap mode allows only two tones in your image: black and white. Bitmap is useful for working with black line art.

Grayscale mode allows you to work with a range of grays from black to white, but no colors. Converting a color image to Grayscale can give the image an old-fashioned look and also reduces the file size.

Indexed Color mode can include a wide range of colors, but can only include a maximum of 256 of these colors in an image. To save an image in the GIF format, you must first convert it to Indexed Color mode.

① Click Image.

② Click Mode.

③ Click an image mode.

In this example, Grayscale is selected. This option brings up a dialog box asking whether or not the user wants to discard color information.

④ Click OK.

Elements converts the image to the new mode.

Fine-tune color with an
ADJUSTMENT LAYER

You can apply complex color and tonal changes to your image with adjustment layers. Adjustment layers appear in the Layers palette, along with the other types of layers in your image. These layers allow you to make changes in hue, brightness, and other image characteristics. When you use adjustment layers, you have the flexibility to fine-tune or even remove your changes later by altering the adjustment layers settings. You can double-click the adjustment layer thumbnail to open the appropriate dialog box.

An adjustment layer affects the underlying layers in the Layers palette. This means that you can affect

multiple layers in an image with a single color or tonal adjustment layer. This is unlike standard color and tonal adjustments that you perform through menu commands, which only affect the currently selected layer.

You can control the intensity of an adjustment layer using the Opacity slider in the Layers palette. For example, if you want to reduce the color or tonal change of an adjustment layer by half, you can simply decrease its opacity to 50%.

CREATE AN ADJUSTMENT LAYER

① Click the Create Adjustment Layer icon.

② Click the adjustment layer you want.

The top menu section lists fill layer types, including Solid Color and Gradient.

The bottom three menu sections list adjustment layer types, including Levels and Threshold.

The adjustment layer dialog box appears.

③ Click and drag the sliders to specify the adjustments you want for the layer.

This example uses Hue/Saturation to brighten the colors in the photo.

④ Click OK.

● The new adjustment layer appears in the Layers palette.

The adjustment layer affects the layers below it.

● You can double-click the layer thumbnail to change the adjustment settings.

DECREASE THE ADJUSTMENT LAYER EFFECT

① Click the adjustment layer.

② Click here to display the Opacity slider.

③ Click and drag the Opacity slider to the left.

The adjustment layer effect is reduced, muting the colors in the image.

Did You Know?

You can click the Eye icon in the Layers palette next to an adjustment layer to hide it and temporarily remove the layer effect. You can also delete an adjustment layer if you want to remove the effect permanently.

Customize It!

If you want to create an adjustment layer that affects only part of your image, select the area before creating your adjustment layer. Elements adds a mask to your adjustment layer affecting only the part of the image that you selected.

Did You Know?

You can apply an Invert adjustment layer to invert the colors in your image, thus turning the image into a photonegative. You can also apply Invert adjustment layers to a selection of an image.

PREVIEW AN IMAGE
for printing

You can preview your image in the Print Preview dialog box to see how it should print on paper. The dialog box displays information such as the orientation of the image, and the size of the margins between the image and the edges of the page. The final appearance of the image on the page depends on its size in pixels, its resolution, and the settings of your printer.

In the dialog box, you can adjust the layout of the image by clicking and dragging handles on the

corners of the image, or by changing the distance from the top and left sides of the page. You can rotate the image 90 degrees in either direction with rotate buttons, for better proportionate fit to the page. You can also add a colored border to the image, based on its print size.

Keep in mind that the changes you make in the Print Preview dialog box only affect how the image prints, not the actual size of the image in pixels.

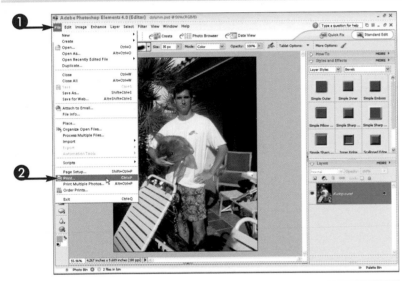

① Click File.

② Click Print.

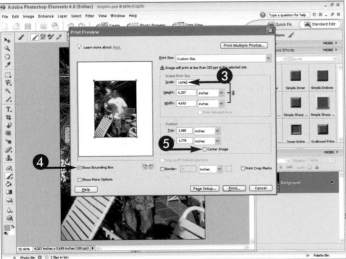

The Print Preview dialog box appears.

③ Type a percentage in the Scale box to scale the image up or down.

④ To reposition the image on the page, click Show Bounding Box (☐ changes to ☑).

⑤ Click Center Image to allow repositioning of the image (☑ changes to ☐).

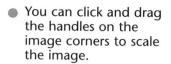

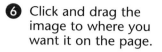

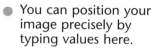

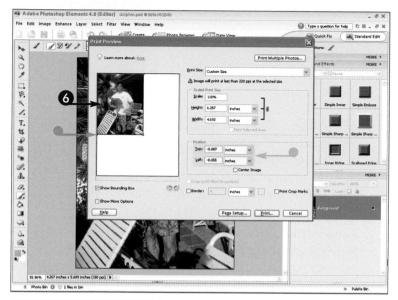

- You can click and drag the handles on the image corners to scale the image.

6 Click and drag the image to where you want it on the page.

- You can position your image precisely by typing values here.

DIFFICULTY LEVEL

46

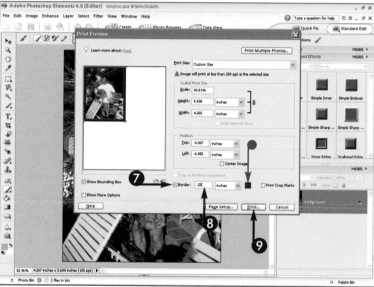

7 Click here to activate the Border option (☐ changes to ✓).

8 Type a width value for the border.

- You can click here to select a custom color.

9 Click Print.

Elements prints your image as it appears in the Print Preview window.

TIPS

Customize It!

You can maximize the size of your printed image by clicking the Fit to Page selection in the Print Size drop-down box. Elements scales the image to the edge of the printed page. You can also choose from multiple preset image-size selections from the Print Size drop-down menu. This menu contains commonly used photo print sizes.

Customize It!

You can automatically add a caption to your printed image by clicking the Show More Options check box and then clicking the Caption check box. Elements inserts any caption information that you have entered in the File Info dialog box below your image. For more information, see Task #49.

Save images for
WEB PUBLISHING

You can save an image file in JPEG or GIF format for publishing on the Web. JPEG format is most suitable for photographs and other images with continuous tones because the format supports millions of colors in a single image. GIF format supports up to 256 colors in a single image and is more suitable for solid-color illustrations or photographs with fewer colors.

When you save an image in the JPEG format, you can specify a quality setting for the image — the

higher the quality, the larger the file size. The JPEG format is ideal for compressing image data to create compact image files.

With the GIF format, you can specify the number of colors in the image, up to a total of 256. The more colors in your image, the higher the quality and the larger the resulting file size. The GIF format can also store multiple image frames in a single GIF image and animate those frames when the GIF is loaded. For more information about animation, see Task #48.

SAVE A JPEG IMAGE

① Click File.

② Click Save for Web.

The Save For Web dialog box appears.

③ Click here and select JPEG.

④ Click here and select JPEG quality settings.

● You can view the size and quality of the resulting JPEG file here.

⑤ Click OK.

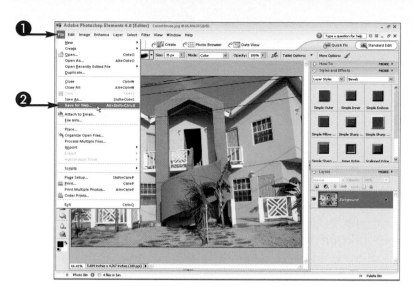

SAVE A GIF IMAGE

1️⃣ Click File.

2️⃣ Click Save for Web.

SAVE A GIF IMAGE

(## 47)

DIFFICULTY LEVEL

The Save For Web dialog box appears.

3️⃣ Click here and select GIF.

4️⃣ Click here and select the number of colors you want to include in the image.

Note: *Because GIF limits images to 256 colors, you may see the quality of your image degrade.*

● You can view the size and quality of the resulting GIF file here.

5️⃣ Click OK.

TIPS

Did You Know?

JPEG is called a *lossy* file format because there is a loss of some image information when you save an image in this format. How much information is lost depends on the quality setting that you choose — the lower the quality, the greater the information loss. This information loss can show up as pixelization in the final JPEG image.

Did You Know?

If your image contains transparent areas, you can select the Transparency check box to retain transparency in the saved GIF file. The GIF format supports transparency, but not semitransparency. Any semitransparent pixels, such as those on the curved edge of objects, convert to a solid color.

Create a
GIF ANIMATION

You can create a multilayered image file in Elements and save it as an animated GIF image. Each layer in the image becomes a frame in the animation. *Frames* are snapshots that show an animated object in different positions, like pages in a flip book.

A GIF animation is an effective way to add motion to your Web pages. It is an easy-to-use alternative to more advanced animation tools such as Flash and Java. Practically all Web browsers can display GIF animations, so you can be sure that most of your Web audience should be able to see them.

Just like a regular GIF image, a GIF animation can only include 256 colors in all of its frames. For this reason, GIF animations should be created using flat-color art rather than continuous-tone photographs.

Elements enables you to specify the duration of each frame in the animation and whether the animation automatically repeats after finishing. Adjusting the frame rate helps you ensure that your animation plays smoothly.

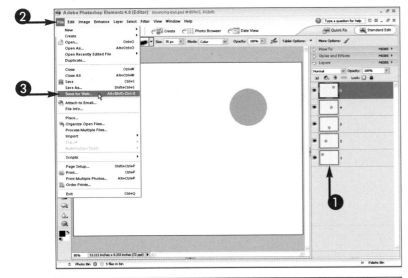

CREATE A GIF ANIMATION

1 Create a series of animation frames, placing each frame in a separate layer.

Each layer should display the animated object in a different position.

The first animation frame is the bottom-most layer.

2 Click File.

3 Click Save for Web.

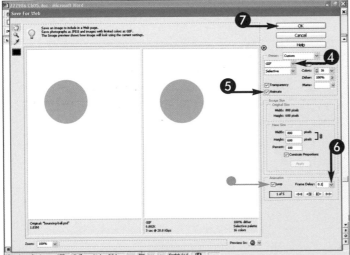

The Save For Web dialog box appears.

4 Click here and select GIF.

5 Click Animate (☐ changes to ☑).

● You can click Loop to make the animation repeat.

6 Click here and select a frame delay.

7 Click OK.

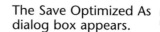
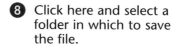
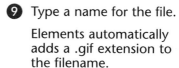
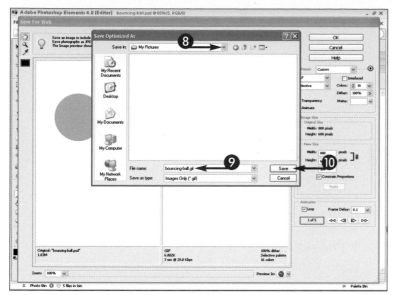

The Save Optimized As dialog box appears.

⑧ Click here and select a folder in which to save the file.

⑨ Type a name for the file.

Elements automatically adds a .gif extension to the filename.

⑩ Click Save.

Elements saves the animated GIF file.

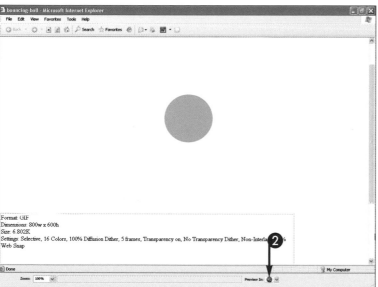

Format: GIF
Dimensions: 800w x 600h
Size: 6.802K
Settings: Selective, 16 Colors, 100% Diffusion Dither, 5 frames, Transparency on, No Transparency Dither, Non-Interlaced, 0%
Web Snap

PREVIEW THE ANIMATION

① Repeat steps **1** to **6**.

② In the Save For Web dialog box, click the Preview In button.

The GIF animation opens in the Web browser and plays.

General information about the image file displays below the image.

Did You Know?

Because GIF animations involve multiple image frames, they can often result in large file sizes. It is important to check the Preview window in the Save For Web dialog box to ensure that the file size is not too large. You can reduce the file size by decreasing the number of colors used in the GIF, or by reducing the number of frames in the animation.

Did You Know?

Frame speeds can vary across different computer systems. If possible, it is a good idea to test your finished animations on a variety of platforms and Web browsers.

ADD INFORMATION
to your image file

You can store caption and copyright information with your Elements image. You may find this useful if you plan to sell or license your images, and want the files to retain information about authorship.

Adding caption information is convenient if you are planning to use some of the other features in Elements. For example, you can automatically add caption and filename information to your printouts through the Print dialog box. See Task #46 for more information.

You can also enter and edit other information, such as a description of the image, so that you can remember settings or situations, or share instructions for multiple users of the same file.

You can also view information about the original camera and settings used to shoot the image. Most recent digital cameras automatically assign the brand name and type of camera, as well as recording any date and time information, shutter speed, and dimensions. Elements places all of this information from the saved image into the File Info dialog box.

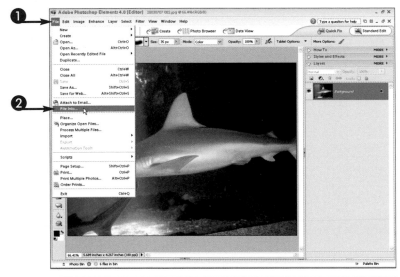

① Click File.

② Click File Info.

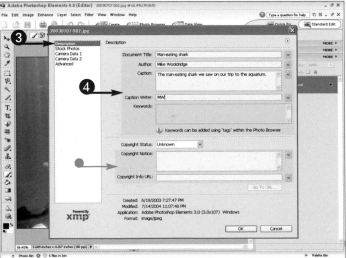

The File Info dialog box appears.

③ Click Description.

The Description area appears.

④ Type the description information for your image.

Select Copyrighted Work to display a copyright symbol in the image window title bar.

● You can add a copyright notice or a Web address that you want to associate with the image.

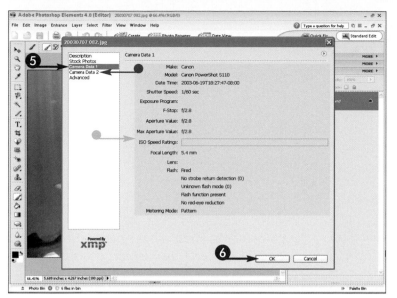

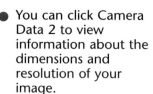

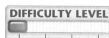

5 Click Camera Data 1.

● The Camera Data 1 area appears, displaying information about the camera and shooting conditions.

● You can click Camera Data 2 to view information about the dimensions and resolution of your image.

6 Click OK.

DIFFICULTY LEVEL

The information is stored with your image.

TIPS

Did You Know?

You can also review key words that are assigned to the image from Organizer. This can help you to find and organize this image or similar images. For more information about assigning key words, known as Tags in Organizer, see Task #74.

Customize It!

By clicking the pop-up menu arrow in the upper right-hand corner, you can save copyright information or a frequently used description as a template for future use. After you save it, you can open a new image by clicking the pop-up menu arrow and loading the template; Elements assigns all settings to the new File Info dialog box.

Print to
PDF FORMAT

You can now easily convert your images and digital creations to PDF format. PDF was created by Adobe, and is recognized worldwide as a universal file format that allows excellent compression and clarity in text, images, and graphics. Because anyone can download the Acrobat Reader for free from www.adobe.com, this format allows others to view your files even if they do not have the original software with which you created the image.

For Elements users, saving to the PDF format allows for smaller, easier-to-manage files that are of print quality. Most printers can print a PDF file, which makes Acrobat an extremely useful tool for digital photographers to print their work professionally. You can also open any PDF format file in Elements, allowing you to work on different platforms. For example, you can receive a brochure layout that is saved in Microsoft Publisher in PDF format, open it, add your photographic edits in Elements, and resave the document in PDF format for printing.

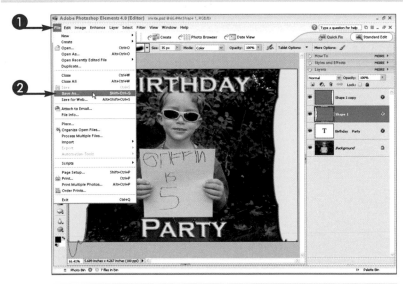

① Click File.

② Click Save As.

③ Click here to open the Format drop-down menu.

④ Click Photoshop PDF.

⑤ Type a filename.

⑥ Click Save.

DIFFICULTY LEVEL

The Save Adobe PDF dialog box appears.

⑦ Specify the PDF options you want.

⑧ Click Save PDF.

Elements saves your file in PDF format.

TIPS

Did You Know?

When you use the Save As feature to save your PDF file, you can click the Layers option (○ changes to ◉) to retain the original layers and editability. You can also use the Print feature to print the image into a PDF format file without actually printing the image.

Caution!

When you open a PDF file that was saved in another program, Elements opens the file and immediately prompts you for a file size and resolution. It then rasterizes the PDF into an image, instead of an editable text or layout file. Be sure to work on a duplicate of the original PDF, in order to ensure that you can edit the text or layout of any design projects.

Speeding Things Up

Keeping things on time and moving smoothly is very important in any workflow or project. People are constantly looking for tools and methods to help them increase their efficiency. Photoshop Elements offers a wide variety of tips and tricks that help you to speed up your workflow, improve the performance of your system, and optimize your results. The whole point is to customize your computer and the Elements setup to improve the way that you manage your workflow.

Over time, your system and software may become sluggish and cumbersome. For example, unused data on a clipboard and fragmented hard drives can cause your computer to run much more slowly, resulting in limited resources and jumbled storage space

being available to Elements. Cluttered screens and disorganized filing can also slow down the system, which must work more slowly because of the additional steps that you need to follow when you navigate around the program and images.

You can use the tasks in this chapter to ensure that your projects go faster and your machine works more smoothly. You can apply some of these tricks within Elements, and others in your operating system, but they all help your work performance. Even simple tricks such as arranging your files can help reduce processing time. You can also save a lot of searching time by organizing your images into descriptive folders to enable you to quickly locate images.

Top 100

INCREASE AVAILABLE RAM
for Elements 4

You can dramatically improve the speed and performance of Elements by customizing the amount of available Random Access Memory, or RAM, and by adjusting the use of cache memory. RAM is perhaps the single most important performance enhancer for Elements 4.

You can specify a percentage amount of available RAM for use within Elements. By default, 50 percent of your computer's available RAM is assigned to Elements. You can also adjust the amount of cache memory to reduce or increase the amount of RAM that Elements uses to store thumbnails and other software files for quick retrieval later.

If you find that your system is running slowly, but you have plenty of memory, Elements has different ways for you to free up that memory. For example, you can clear your History states, clipboard, and cache memory in order to immediately re-use your computer's assigned memory. However, keep in mind that clearing is irreversible, and any information that you clear is permanently lost. You should be particularly careful with History states, which are a great benefit when working on difficult projects.

① Click Edit.

② Click Preferences.

③ Click Memory & Image Cache.

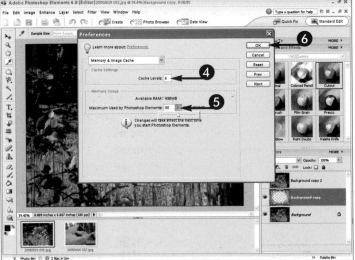

The Preferences dialog box appears.

④ Type the number of cache levels you want.

Higher cache levels use more memory.

⑤ Type a number, or click and drag the slider, to set the amount of memory that is used by Elements.

⑥ Click OK.

7 Click Edit.

8 Click Clear.

9 Click the category you want to clear.

Note: Clearing is irreversible.

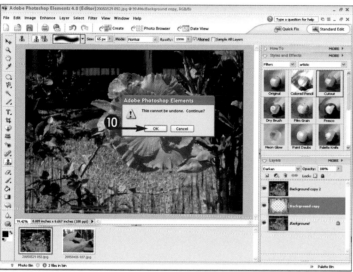

A dialog box appears, verifying that you want to clear.

10 Click OK.

Elements empties the memory cache you selected.

TIPS

Did You Know?

Ideally, you should have no less than 256MB of RAM available on your computer for Elements to run. In fact, you can assign up to 2GB of RAM to your computer.

Did You Know?

Every running program, including your operating system, uses RAM. If your machine has limited RAM, then running other programs with Elements may reduce your RAM to dangerously low amounts and cause your machine to lock up or run very slowly. If you have limited RAM, be sure to run Elements 4 alone whenever possible to speed up its processing power. If you must open multiple programs, then open Elements first, to assign it the highest available RAM percentage possible.

Improve performance with
SCRATCH DISKS

Scratch disks are hard drives or storage units that Elements uses as temporary memory when all available RAM is used up. When you work in Elements, it treats your hard drive like a memory cache. If you only use one drive, then that drive divides its speed between multiple functions at once, which slows down the processing speed. By using a different hard drive as your scratch disk, Elements can use much more space for working with large files or complex filters, thus speeding up performance. As a result, a scratch disk is almost as important as RAM memory for smooth processing.

You can easily set up your scratch disk. By default, the scratch disk is set to the C: drive when you install Elements in Windows. However, you can edit this setting and assign a different hard drive. For example, you can make the scratch disk a different drive, so that when Elements applies a filter to an image on one drive, it can use the second drive for other functions and not interfere or have to wait on the first drive to stop processing.

1 Click Edit.

2 Click Preferences.

3 Click Plug-Ins & Scratch Disks.

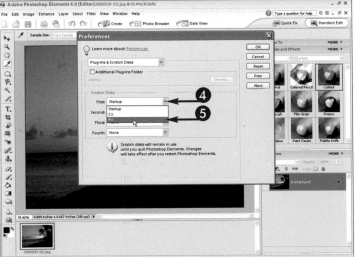

The Preferences dialog box appears.

4 Click here to view available drives.

5 Select a scratch disk drive.

6 Click here and select an additional scratch disk.

● Elements can register up to four scratch disks.

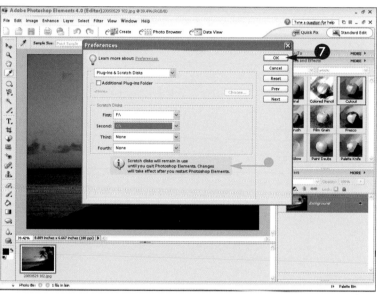

7 Click OK.

● The scratch disk becomes effective the next time your start up Elements.

TIPS

Customize It!

When you have only one hard drive available on your computer, Elements defaults to it. However, there is a process called *partitioning* that involves splitting off a section of the hard drive and transforming it into a recognizable second drive that you can assign as a scratch disk.

Caution!

Partitioning involves dividing a single drive into multiple virtual drives. A mistake during partitioning can destroy all files and programs on the drive you use for all of your computer functions and Windows. If you are not experienced in partitioning a hard drive, then before you start, you should consult your operating system's instructions. You may also want to contact a professional computer technician.

DEFRAGMENT
to speed up your computer

If you are using Windows, then you can improve system performance by using a standard Windows tool, the Disk Defragmenter. Defragmenting helps the computer to access data more quickly.

When you save an image to a hard drive, you are saving the information on little spaces called *bits*. On a fragmented hard drive, these bits may not be located next to each other. This is because, if there is not enough adjacent disk space, Windows divides the file into segments and stores each of these segments wherever it can fit them.

Windows knows where all of the segments are and in what order it must retrieve them, but having to search in multiple locations for file segments and then having to run the reassembled file can slow your computer down. In Elements, you may often work with files that are at least 20 to 40MB in size. When the hard drive stores a file of that size, it may have to break it up into several segments and scatter them across the drive, which slows the system down even more.

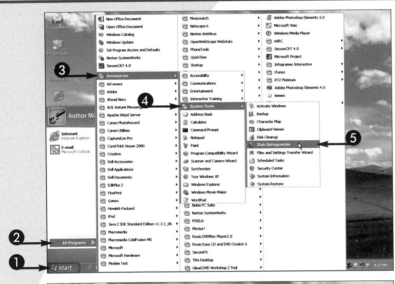

① Click Start.

② Click All Programs.

③ Click Accessories.

④ Click System Tools.

⑤ Click Disk Defragmenter.

The Disk Defragmenter window appears.

⑥ Click the drive that you want to defragment.

⑦ Click Analyze.

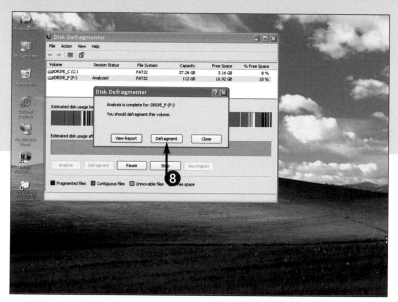

A dialog box appears, recommending whether or not to defragment the drive you have selected.

⑧ Click Defragment.

A dialog box informs you when defragmentation is complete.

● Click Close to shut down Disk Defragmenter.

● Click View Report to see details about the defragmentation.

TIPS

Did You Know?

Removing unused programs is a good way to improve the speed of your operating system. If you have many unused files, then whenever you install new ones, the chance of fragmenting your drive increases, thus slowing performance. Defragment your system regularly to keep the drive more compact. There is also commercial software available that do excellent digital housekeeping to keep your system running faster.

Try It!

You can use permanent back-up storage for important data or if you have a lot of files that you want to archive. The price of a CD-ROM has dropped to the point where burning disks is no longer cost-prohibitive. The introduction of DVD-R media allows you to store even more data onto a single disk.

CALIBRATE
your monitor

When working with graphics projects, you need to ensure that the colors that you see on-screen are accurate and consistent with the results you want. You can obtain more accurate colors in Elements by using the Adobe Gamma Correction tool. This tool uses a Wizard interface to calibrate your monitor to the correct International Color Consortium (ICC) color profile to ensure that the color profile is suitable for your monitor and shows the colors most accurately.

You should calibrate your monitor using the light conditions in which you normally work. These conditions dramatically influence how color displays on your monitor.

The Gamma Correction tool has several methods for you to adjust and create your ICC color profile. Calibrating your monitor involves adjusting brightness, contrast, and gamma colors, as well as selecting the *white point*, which is the point where your monitor recognizes the total sum of all colors, or white. Many of the wizard screens recognize hardware preferences and default settings, but you can change these settings and save the final color result under a custom name.

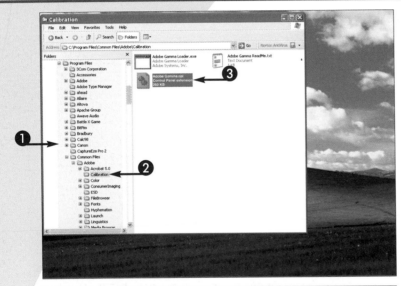

① Open Windows Explorer.

② Navigate through the folder to Calibration.

You can also click Program Files, Common Files, Adobe, and then Calibration.

③ Double-click Adobe Gamma.cpl.

The Adobe Gamma dialog box appears.

④ Click the Step By Step (Wizard) option (○ changes to ◉).

⑤ Click Next.

The Adobe Gamma wizard appears and guides you through the steps.

DIFFICULTY LEVEL

⑥ Proceed through the steps, clicking Continue, until you reach the last page.

⑦ Toggle between the Before and After options to compare your previous color settings to your new color settings (○ changes to ◉).

⑧ Click Finish.

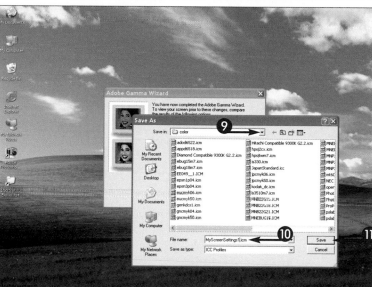

The Save As dialog box appears.

⑨ Click here and navigate to the folder where you want to save the profile.

⑩ Type a profile name.

⑪ Click Save.

Elements saves your new color profile and assigns it to your monitor.

TIPS

Customize It!
You can find more color files for custom monitor calibration. There are numerous files in the Color folder where you found the Adobe Gamma Calibration folder. You can create your own file or load a saved one. Businesses sometimes have a specific ICC color profile designed for their own brand recognition and company colors. If you do print work, some printers may require you to supply your own color file for print to guarantee color quality.

Did You Know?
You can access additional color profiles on your monitor's installation disks. Browse through the disks to locate additional profiles that you can load through Adobe Gamma. You can also find additional color profiles at your monitor manufacturer's website. Check your monitor's manuals for website or additional information.

MAXIMIZE
your workspace

Even if you have a very large monitor, you can still fit only so much information on-screen, and graphics work always seems to require more visual space. You can maximize your workspace in Elements by arranging toolbars and palettes on-screen to make the most out of the limited available space.

You can maximize your Elements workspace in several ways. For example, the new Palette Bin allows you to merge your individual palettes into one area, which you can hide instantly or resize to increase the available on-screen workspace.

Another new feature is the Photo Bin, which shows all open image documents. You can hide and display this feature with a mouse click, as well as resize it. As a result, you can use this feature to increase your workspace area and to speed up your workflow.

Regardless of how you arrange your workspace, you should find an arrangement that works for you and then use it consistently. Familiarity with the setup is an important factor in increasing your productivity.

HIDE BINS

1 Click the Close Palette Bin button (▶).

2 Click the Close Photo Bin button (▼).

Elements hides the palettes on the edge of the screen.

● You can click the Open Palette Bin button (◀) to reveal the Palette Bin again.

● You can click the Open Photo Bin button (▲) to reveal the Photo Bin again.

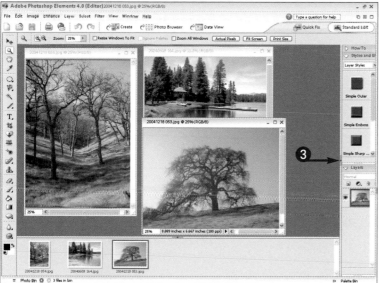

CHANGE PALETTE SIZE

① Position the mouse cursor over the edge of the Palette Bin or Photo Bin.

The cursor changes to a double arrow resize (◀▐▶).

② Click and drag the edge to adjust the size of the palette.

Elements resizes the palette as you move the cursor.

③ Release the mouse button when the palette is the size you want.

TIPS

Customize It!

You can use several other simple tricks that can help you to maximize your Elements workspace. For example, by clicking the Window menu, you can display and hide any on-screen palette or bin. Also, if you have any free-floating palettes, then you can press the Tab key to remove them from the screen. When you press it again, they reappear in their last locations.

Apply It!

You can undock the main toolbar by clicking the top of the toolbar just above the Move tool, and dragging the toolbar away from the left-hand side of the screen. The toolbar becomes a free-floating two-column toolbar that you can move anywhere on-screen.

Increase your
SCREEN RESOLUTION

Sometimes you can work more efficiently when you have multiple images open at the same time by increasing the resolution settings of your monitor. A resolution of 1024 pixels wide by 768 pixels tall is just large enough to view Elements' entire Toolbox and Options Bar settings. But switching the resolution to higher settings can give you more room in your workspace to display images, even when Elements' palettes are open.

You can increase your monitor resolution in the Display Properties dialog box located in the Windows

Control Panel. The dialog box also allows you to control the color quality of your monitor, set color schemes for windows and buttons, and change the desktop background image.

The resolution setting that is best for you will depend to some extent on the physical size of your monitor. Some of the higher resolutions available in the Windows Control Panel may only be useable on larger monitors — for instance, those that are 19" or larger in size.

❶ Click Start.

❷ Click Control Panel.

The Control Panel window opens.

❸ Click Appearance and Themes.

The Appearance and Themes window opens.

❹ Click Display.

The Display Properties dialog box opens.

❺ Click the Settings tab.

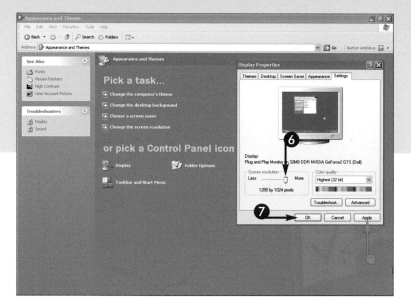

6 Click and drag the Screen Resolution slider to the right to select a higher resolution.

● You can click Apply to preview the new resolution.

7 Click OK.

#56

DIFFICULTY LEVEL

In this example, the screen resolution has been changed to 1280 pixels wide by 800 pixels tall.

TIPS

Did You Know?

You can use the Display Properties dialog box to change your monitor's color quality, which is determined by the number of colors it displays. For best results when using Adobe Photoshop Elements, make sure the color quality is at its highest setting. You can find the color quality menu under the Settings tab.

Customize It!

You can create custom desktop images—also known as wallpaper—in Photoshop Elements to personalize the workspace on your PC. To apply a custom desktop image, click the Desktop tab in the Display Properties dialog box and then click Browse to locate the image on your computer. For best results, make sure the resolution of your wallpaper image is the same as that of your monitor.

USE RECIPES
to speed up common tasks

You can speed up some everyday tasks with the Recipes feature in the How To palette. The How To palette contains a group of instructional tutorials, or recipes, that guide you through certain tasks. You can choose from a wide variety of topics, from Web page design to color correction on an image.

Each recipe appears in a step-by-step format that you can follow through the entire task. The How To menu also displays available options, and provides links to other recipes that are related to the recipe on which you are working.

You can also speed up your recipes with the How To palette's automatic completion feature. Many steps within the recipes have a Play button next to the text, When you click the Play button, Elements either completes the step automatically or opens the appropriate dialog box for you to customize the results of the step. This feature is a very handy time saver when you use this palette.

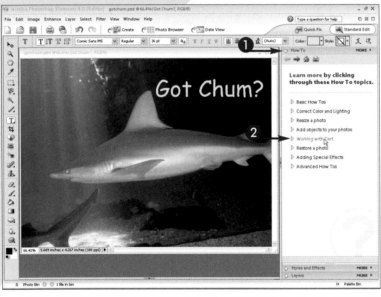

1 Click the How To palette.

2 Click a How To topic.

● The How To topic expands, showing multiple How To tasks.

3 Select a How To task.

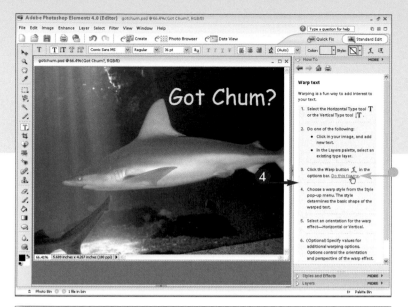

The task steps appear in the How To palette.

④ Follow the steps to complete the recipe.

● You can click the *Do this for me* hyperlinks to have Elements automatically complete some steps for you.

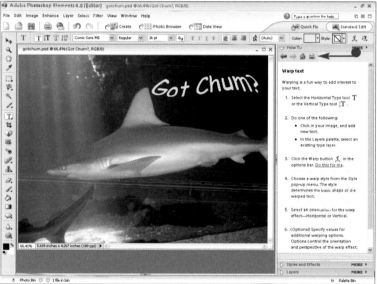

Your image displays the results of the How To you selected.

● You can click here to navigate the How To palette.

TIPS

Did You Know?
You can also download more tutorials to use in Photoshop Elements 4 directly from Adobe. Elements provides access to these tutorials through the Help drop-down menu. Click Photoshop Elements Online. Your browser will open to the Photoshop Elements website. You can select helpful tutorials to continue learning new methods and tricks.

Did You Know?
The How To palette has navigational buttons across the top of the palette that allow you to move back and forth between How To pages and menus that you have already visited in the palette. This is useful for retracing your steps if you used multiple tasks or if you want to review a process that you used earlier.

AUTOMATE
file conversions

Some tasks, such as downloading images from a digital camera, involve changing many images from one file type to another. For example, many digital photographers today convert their images from TIF format to JPG format. A digital camera commonly holds from 50 to 200 images, and so having to convert them one by one can be very tedious and time-consuming. You can use the Process Multiple Files utility to turn this task from a repetitive chore into a quick and easy process.

The Process Multiple Files dialog box takes all images from a selected folder, applies the conversion to every acceptable image format in that folder, and then saves the images in a destination folder in the new format. You can set up your source and destination folders in advance to ensure that your images are always saved where you want them. After you establish the settings for the file conversion, Elements then does all of the work for you, and in a lot less time.

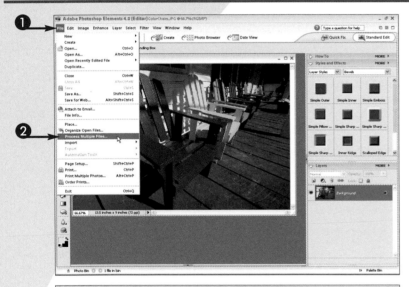

① Click File.

② Click Process Multiple Files.

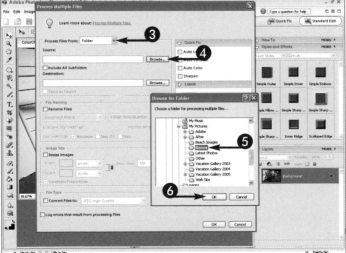

The Process Multiple Files dialog box appears.

③ Click here and select your source type.

④ In the Source area, click Browse to open the Browse for Folder dialog box.

⑤ Navigate to and select the source folder.

⑥ Click OK.

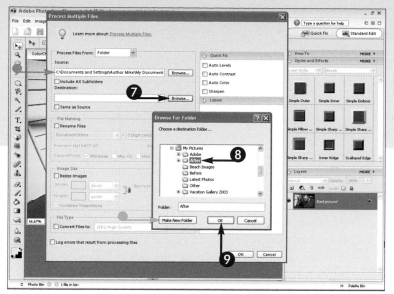

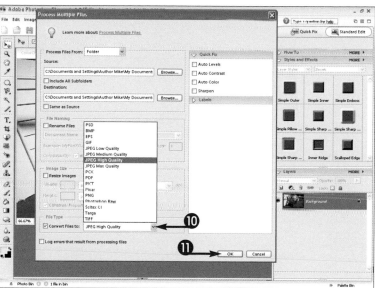

- Elements sets the folder you selected as the source folder.

⑦ In the Destination area, click Browse to open the Browse For Folder dialog box.

⑧ Navigate to and select the destination folder.

- If you like, you can create a new folder as your destination folder.

⑨ Click OK to close the Browse For Folder dialog box.

⑩ Click here and select a conversion file format.

⑪ Click OK.

The Process Multiple Files dialog box closes.

Elements converts your files.

TIPS

Caution!

Keep in mind that when processing multiple photos, this feature converts every file that it finds within the designated source to the specified format, even for those files that do not require it. You should ensure that the source location only contains those files that you want to convert in order to avoid unnecessary conversions and duplicate files.

Customize It!

Processing multiple files is a great way to save time removing images from your digital camera. For example, if your digital camera has a large number of TIF photos that you want to save as more compact JPG photos, connect the camera to the computer, and directly denote the camera as your source folder in the Process Multiple Files dialog box.

AUTOMATE
other details in batches

You can use the Process Multiple Files dialog box to automate more than just file conversions. For example, you may have a large batch of images that you need to resize as thumbnails for a website, where the thumbnails also need to be a specific height or width. You can enter the height or width that you want the final images to be, and even specify a higher image resolution in case the conversion is for print, and the Process Multiple Files dialog box does the rest.

You can also rename files using the Process Multiple Files dialog box. This dialog box allows you to make minor changes to a filename when you apply other changes to the image, as a way of differentiating between two similar files. Elements lists common extensions in a drop-down menu and shows examples of the resulting filename as it will appear with the selected extensions. Elements offers plenty of different types of extensions for your files.

① Click File.

② Click Process Multiple Files.

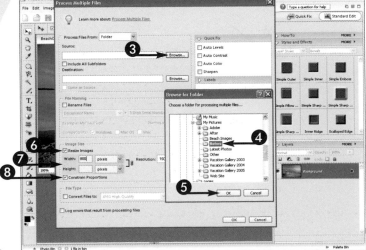

The Process Multiple Files dialog box appears.

③ In the Source area, click Browse.

④ In the Browse for Folder dialog box, navigate to the source folder.

⑤ Click OK.

⑥ If you want to change the size of the images, select the Resize Images option (☐ changes to ☑).

⑦ Set your resize settings.

⑧ If Constrain Proportions is selected, you only need to type either the width or height for size.

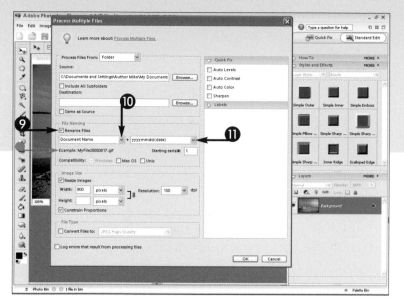

9 If you want to rename the files, click the Rename Files option (☐ changes to ☑).

10 Click here and select a document naming scheme.

11 Click here and select a secondary naming scheme.

● Elements displays how the name appears with the extensions you have selected.

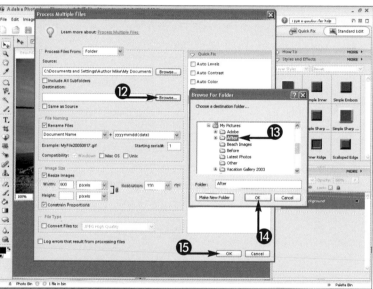

12 Click Browse.

13 In the Browse For Folder dialog box, navigate to the destination folder.

14 Click OK.

15 Click OK to close the Process Multiple Files dialog box.

Elements processes your files.

TIPS

Caution!
When performing file conversions, keep in mind that several file formats, including JPG, are considered *lossy* formats, meaning that each time you save the file, it loses detail due to the compression technique. If detail is important, use the TIF format. The file size is larger, but the TIF format is lossless, and maintains the original detail.

Apply It!
When renaming files, be as descriptive as possible. Poorly chosen filenames, such as numeric filenames with date extensions, can make it difficult to differentiate between files. Keep the original filenames descriptive so that when you run a batch process on the files, you have more flexibility if you need to add a code-like numeric extension.

ORGANIZE
your images in Elements

Using the Open method in the File menu to locate and open an image can be very time-consuming. Similarly, not having easy access to critical information about an image can also slow you down. Fortunately, Elements has two built-in features that can help you quickly find images and embed information in an image.

Elements Organizer lets you easily catalog large numbers of digital photos, then browse, sort, and filter them. It also enables you to create your own organization scheme by labeling your photos with user-defined tags. You can easily switch back and forth between the Elements Editor and Organizer.

The File Info menu option allows you to input certain information into your file. For example, you can type your personal information, descriptions, copyright information, and even website URL. If you type copyright information, the copyright symbol appears in the title bar when you view the image. When you add information to your image, any program that recognizes embedded information will allow users to view this information.

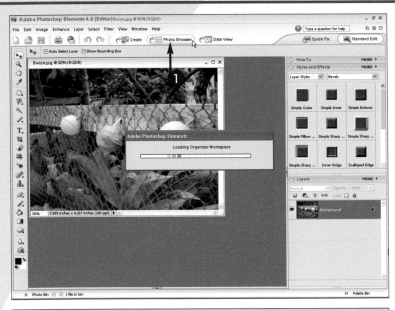

SWITCH TO ORGANIZER

① Click Photo Browser.

Elements opens Organizer.

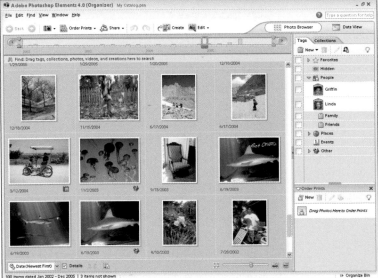

The photos in your collection are arranged in a grid.

Note: *For more information about Organizer, see Chapter 8.*

The File Info dialog box appears.

3 Type your information.

● If you select Copyrighted Work in the Copyright Status field, the title bar will display the copyright symbol.

4 Click OK.

When you save the file, Elements embeds the information you entered.

TIPS

Did You Know?

There are other ways to open Elements Organizer. You can click either View and Organize Photos or Make Photo Creations in the welcome screen that appears when you start Elements. You can also select Organizer under the Start Up In menu of the welcome screen to automatically launch Organizer when you start the program.

Did You Know?

When adding tags to photos in Elements Organizer, the tags appear as keywords in the File Info dialog box. You can use tags to assign specific and detailed descriptions to your Elements images and projects. For more information about tags, see Task #74.

Chapter 7

Working with Other Elements Tools

In Photoshop Elements 4, you can sometimes achieve the same effect in different ways. This occurs when a class of tools or filters contains items whose capabilities overlap each other. There are also many tools and utilities that fall outside of the regular tool categories, such as selecting, inserting content, and pixel manipulation. Some of these unique features are included in this chapter because, although they do not fit within the other categories, you can use these tools to perform many useful tasks and to create many interesting results.

This chapter discusses features such as the new Elements 4 Photo Bin and Palette Bins, which allow you to quickly access open images and different available palettes, as well as

easily increase your available workspace. You can also see how to scan images, work with tool preset options, and design gradients and graphical patterns. This chapter also shows you how to manage third-party plug-ins. In Chapter 5, you can learn how to open or convert a PDF file into a format that Elements can use, and how to save it again as a PDF.

Each of the tools and tricks in this chapter offer unique benefits and powerful capabilities. Although some may be tools used less frequently than others, they each have quite a bit of functionality to offer users, from the professional to the hobbyist, whatever the size or complexity of project you do.

Top 100

Design
CUSTOM GRADIENTS

You can use the Gradient tool to create graphic effects. From shading an object to creating a metallic appearance, gradients enhance many aspects of a graphic design. You can access many different gradients in the default Gradient tool presets, or you can design your own custom gradients.

You can access the Gradient Editor by clicking inside the gradient sample in the Options bar. The Gradient Editor allows you to edit and save an original gradient to add to the presets in the Options bar. You can

create and edit gradients by adding opacity stops and color stops to the gradient bar. The opacity stops allow you to make sections of a gradient appear semi-transparent. The color stops indicate the colors that you want to blend together in your gradient. By sliding the color stops along the gradient bar, you can affect the way in which adjacent colors blend. The farther apart the colors are, the smoother and longer the blend. By double-clicking a color stop, you can change the color located at that stop.

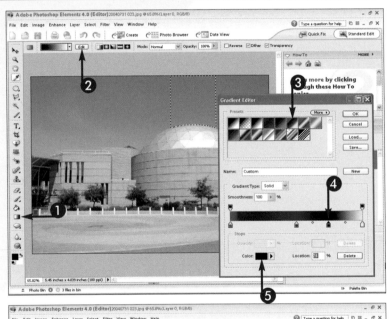

① Click the Gradient tool (▣).

② Click the Edit button to open the Gradient Editor dialog box.

③ Click a gradient in the Presets window.

④ Click the gradient bar to insert a color stop.

To remove a color stop, click and drag the gradient bar off the edge of the Gradient Editor dialog box.

⑤ With a color stop selected, click in the Color box.

The Color Picker dialog box appears for that color stop.

⑥ Select the color you want.

⑦ Click OK.

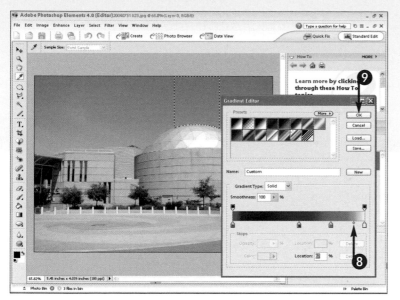

The color you selected appears in the color stop.

8 Slide the Color Midpoint diamond to move the blending midpoint.

Click the gradient bar to add additional color stops and adjustments as needed for your gradient.

9 In the Gradient Editor dialog box, click OK.

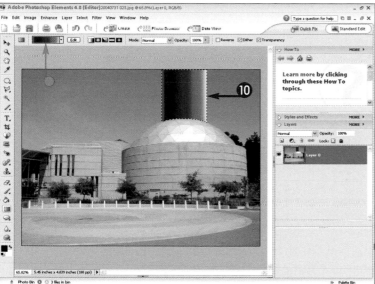

● Elements creates the custom gradient.

10 Click and drag to apply the gradient.

In this example, the gradient is applied inside a selection.

TIPS

Customize It!

You can create a Noise gradient by selecting Noise from the Gradient Type menu in the Gradient Editor dialog box. Noise gradients are so named because Elements uses random noise to calculate the dozens of colors that appear in the resulting gradient. The Roughness setting in the dialog box controls whether the adjacent colors in the gradient are blurred or sharply defined.

Did You Know?

You can save and share gradient files. After you create your new gradients, save them by clicking the Save button in the Gradient Editor dialog box. Elements prompts you to name the gradient, and to browse to the file location where you want to save it. Elements stores gradient files in the C:\Program Files\ Adobe\Photoshop Elements 4.0\Presets\ Gradients folder.

Define and use a
GRAPHIC PATTERN

You can create graphical patterns to use in your projects. You often see patterns in advertisements, art, Web designs, and graphic designs. You can apply patterns in Elements by incorporating them into your layers or selections. You can apply a pattern to an entire image or a simple selection within the image, such as text or a shape. Elements has a package of pre-made patterns that are useful for many types of projects.

You can define custom patterns with almost any graphic, and then use them to create new patterns.

Patterns are often used in website backgrounds and digital graphics, or as a texture for a special shape effect or 3D model. In digital photography, they can be used for cartography, geographical layouts, and sectioning a photo.

After you apply a pattern to an image, you can edit the results just like any simplified graphic. You can easily define a pattern from an image, rectangular selection of an image, or a custom creation using the tools in Elements 4, and then saving the new pattern for use in your graphics.

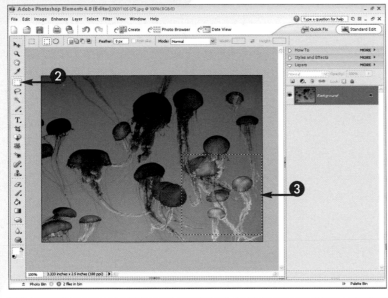

① Open an image.

② Click the Rectangular Marquee tool (▣).

③ Create a selection with the Rectangular Marquee tool.

Note: Elements cannot create a pattern out of shapes or text that have not been simplified.

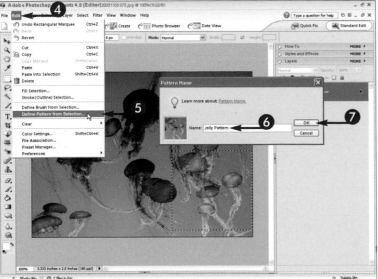

④ Click Edit.

⑤ Click Define Pattern from Selection.

The Pattern Name dialog box opens.

⑥ Type a name for the pattern.

⑦ Click OK.

136

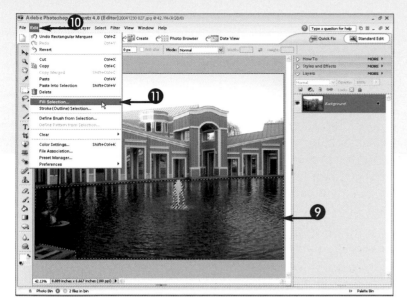

8 Create a new image.

This image should be significantly larger than the pattern selection.

9 Make a selection with a selection tool.

10 Click Edit.

11 Click Fill Selection.

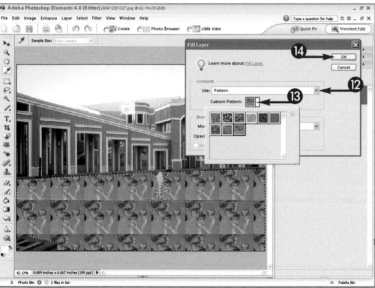

The Fill Layer dialog box appears.

12 Click here and select Pattern.

13 Click here and select a custom pattern from the palette.

14 Click OK.

Elements fills the image with the new pattern as shown in the example.

TIPS

Apply It!

You can easily create a grid. Start by making a small, square document. With the Line tool, draw a one- to three-pixel vertical and horizontal line. Click Edit, then click Define Pattern to set your image as a pattern. When you use the Fill command to fill a document or selection with this pattern, the pattern generates a grid.

Did You Know?

When you scale up a pattern, the pattern may appear grainy. To avoid this, create your pattern in a larger version. You can now resize duplicates of the pattern image to a smaller scale and then define it as a pattern. Repeat these steps until you have a useful range of pattern sizes.

Manage additional
PLUG-INS

You can use dozens of filters and effects in Elements to create amazing results. However, there are other software packages, called third-party plug-ins, which you can also use with Elements. Third-party plug-ins can expand on or create new effects in your graphics. However, because there are so many plug-ins available, they can quickly become disorganized.

You can manage your plug-ins by separating them from the program. By default, Elements stores plug-ins in your Adobe/Elements 4/Plug-ins folder. To keep better track of your plug-ins, you may want

to store them outside of the Elements folder. You can designate a second plug-ins folder to load at startup, so that you can expand your plug-ins outside of Elements and keep them organized.

Using this technique, if you ever need to reinstall Elements, you only have to redefine the secondary plug-ins folder. Because many plug-ins only require being present in a specific folder, maintaining them in a separate location can save time by not having to worry about installing all of your plug-ins again.

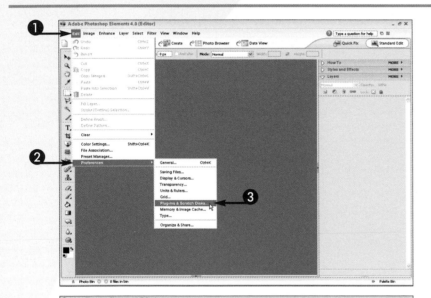

① Click Edit.

② Click Preferences.

③ Click Plug-Ins & Scratch Disks.

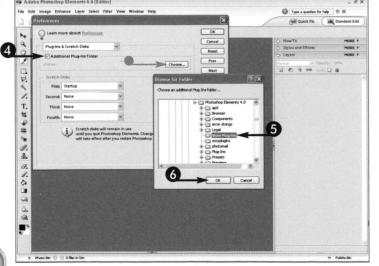

The Preferences dialog box appears.

④ Click the Additional Plug-ins Folder check box (☐ changes to ☑).

Elements opens the Browse for Folder dialog box.

● If you have already defined an additional plug-ins folder, you may have to click Choose to open the Browse for Folder dialog box.

⑤ Select a folder to designate as a secondary plug-ins folder.

⑥ Click OK.

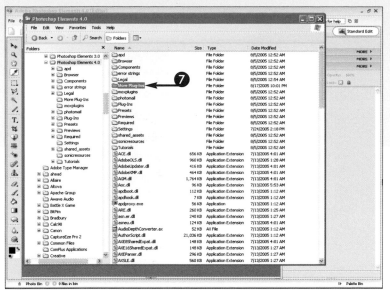

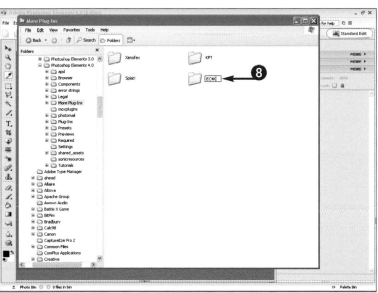

Elements automatically assigns a new folder in Preferences, if necessary.

⑦ Open Windows Explorer and scroll to the secondary plug-ins folder.

 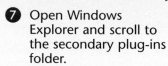 
⑧ In Windows, create additional subfolders for your plug-ins.

To create a new folder from the menu, click File, then New, then Folder.

Some third-party plug-ins will create their own folders during installation.

On the next startup, Elements loads the plug-ins from the new third-party plug-ins folder.

 TIPS

Did You Know?

One very good reason for keeping plug-ins external is safety. If you need to reinstall Elements, then all of your default folders are reset, and you have to reinstall the plug-ins. Filing separately saves time. Some plug-ins require their own software to properly install them, but many can simply be referred to the third-party plug-ins folder. See the plug-ins' installation instructions for more information.

Did You Know?

After installing plug-ins, you must restart Elements to access your new plug-ins. When Elements reads a plug-in, the program places them in the Filters menu, but if the menu becomes too full, Elements places them in the Filters, Other submenu.

Manage your
TOOL PRESETS

When you open tools such as gradients, brushes, and shapes in Elements, you can choose from many variations. You can also add more variations to some of these palettes and tools, as well as delete tools that you no longer need. Elements also makes it easy to track, edit, and reset these preset groups of tool options.

You can use the Preset Manager to customize your tool presets. The Preset Manager is located in the Edit menu. When you open the Preset Manager, a dialog box appears, displaying options for brushes,

color swatches, gradients, and patterns. You can use these option menus to change the available variations for each tool, as well as to import more tools. For example, you can change the current gradient set to a different group of gradients. Other options include changing brushes, patterns, and color swatches. You can save your custom palette layouts to use at another time. If you do not save your custom palette, and you reset the palettes to the default settings, then you lose your custom design.

① Click Edit.

② Click Preset Manager.

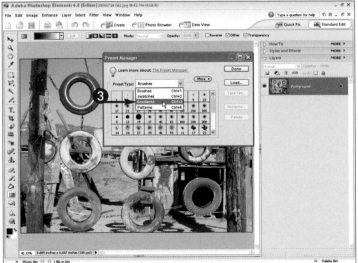

The Preset Manager dialog box appears.

③ Click here and select Gradients.

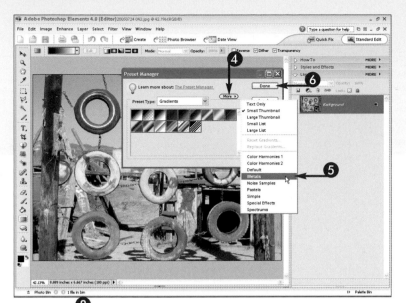

④ Click More.

⑤ Select a new gradient set from the drop-down list.

⑥ Click Done.

64

DIFFICULTY LEVEL

Elements resets the tool palette to reflect the new gradient set.

⑦ Click the Gradient tool ().

⑧ Click the Gradient selection drop-down arrow.

Elements displays the new preset gradient set.

TIPS

Customize It!

You can make changes to your tool presets when using the Preset Manager. To customize your sets, you can choose from options that include delete, rename, save set, and load. You can design a set of your favorite brushes by deleting existing brushes and defining new ones. You can then save the set as a custom brush file. Now you can load your favorite brush set when you need it. To avoid losing the original sets, do not save over the default sets.

Did You Know?

You can import brush sets from outside of Elements. Simply download the ABR format brushes file from its source into the C:\Program Files\Adobe\Photoshop Elements 4.0\Presets\ Brushes folder. Load the new set in the Preset Manager to use the new brushes.

Work with the
TRANSFORM TOOL

You can transform and distort entire images, as well as layer objects. The Free Transform tool allows you to manipulate the shape and scale of your images with your mouse. For example, you can add perspective, distort, and resize your graphics. This tool is also useful when you want to scale an object to fit into a larger or smaller space.

You can find the Free Transform tool in the Image menu. When you click the object that you want to transform, a square bounding box surrounds the object. You can click and drag any of the square

intersection points to scale it. If you press and hold the Ctrl key while you drag, you can skew and distort your object. When you are finished, you can click the Commit button, or double-click the object within the bounding box.

You can transform vector graphics, such as unsimplified text and shapes, without losing the clarity and sharpness of their edges. You can also transform simplified graphics, such as photographs, although excessive transformation may cause loss of clarity and pixelization.

1 Click the object layer.

2 Click Image.

3 Click Transform.

4 Click Free Transform.

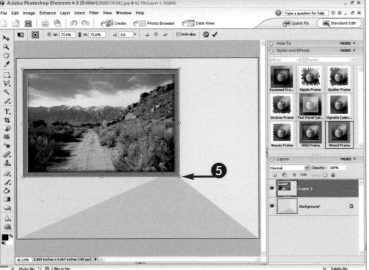

A bounding box with corner and side handles appears around the object.

5 Click and drag a corner handle to scale your object.

You can scale up or down.

To distort your object, press and hold the Ctrl+Shift+Alt keys and drag a corner handle.

To distort your object in perspective, press and hold the Ctrl+Shift+Alt keys and drag a handle.

- To distort using only one handle, just click and drag the handle.

⑥ Click the Commit button to apply your transformations.

Elements applies your transformations.

TIPS

Did You Know?
You can apply equally horizontal or vertical transformations from your object midpoint. If you press and hold the Shift key while scaling, it constrains the proportions to remain equal, and so your image remains proportional to the original size.

Did You Know?
You can free transform any object or layer, except backgrounds. If you try to change a background, a prompt appears asking you to change the background to a layer. Accepting this change enables the effectiveness of the Transformation tool.

Caution!
Although you can scale image selections and simplified images, you should exercise caution when doing so. Scaling a JPG, BMP, or other pixel-based image can result in pixelization and loss of clarity.

EXTRACT AN OBJECT
from a background

You can extract an object in your photo from its background using the Magic Extractor tool. You define the object and background by brushing lines over them, and Elements deletes the background automatically. This tool can be useful for removing complex objects set against the sky, sides of buildings, and other evenly colored backgrounds. Using the Magic Extractor can be quicker than selecting the object with one of the Lasso tools, inverting the selection, and then deleting the background.

To produce the cleanest extraction possible, sample as much of the foreground and background of your image as you can. You can use the other tools in the Magic Extractor dialog box to edit your brush lines and improve your extractions. You can also click the foreground and background boxes to change the colors of the lines that the brushes apply to your image. This can be helpful if colors in your image match the default brush colors.

❶ Click Image.

❷ Click Magic Extractor (▨).

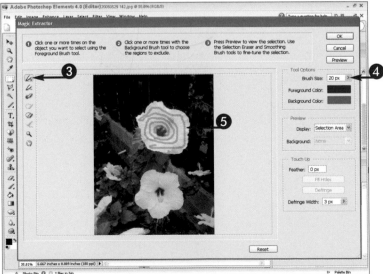

The Magic Extractor dialog box opens.

❸ Click the Foreground Brush tool (▨).

❹ Click here to specify a brush size.

❺ Click and drag to apply brush strokes to the object you want to keep.

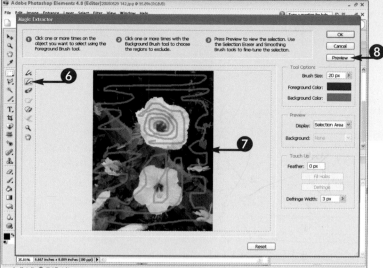

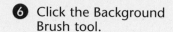

6 Click the Background Brush tool.

7 Click and drag to apply brush lines to the background you want to remove.

8 Click Preview.

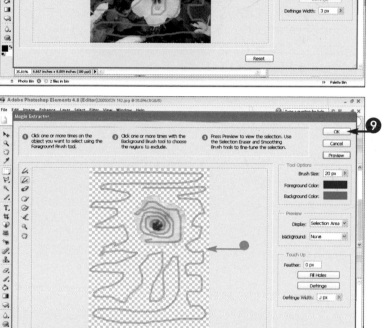

● Elements extracts the object from the background and displays a preview.

To repeat the process, click and hold Alt to change Cancel to Reset, then click Reset.

9 Click OK to complete the extraction and return to your image.

TIPS

Did You Know?

You can use a similar tool called the Magic Selection Brush (![icon]) to create selections by brushing lines across an object in your image. Elements analyzes the pixels covered by the lines and selects the corresponding object in the image. You can use different versions of the tool, available in the Options bar, to add or subtract from your selection.

Did You Know?

Elements offers several different ways to grow or shrink your selections after you make them. For instance, to expand your selection by a set number of pixels, click Select, Modify, and then Expand. To contract your selection, click Select, Modify, and then Contract.

SCAN
in a photo

You can use your scanner to import all of those old photographs into your computer for cleanup, cropping, and reproduction. Scanning is easy, and is a great tool that enables home photographers to digitally preserve their photographs. Most people store boxfuls of photos because they are difficult and expensive to organize into photo albums. With a scanner you can digitize your photos, and use them for distribution on the Web, a slideshow, or in e-mail.

Scanners are also useful for reproducing old or damaged photos, so that you can repair the

scratches, faded areas, and torn edges, and finally reprint them onto high-quality photo paper. This is a wonderful way of keeping old photos alive, and sharing those photos with friends and family.

Although scanners and import software vary from manufacturer to manufacturer, the basic functions are similar. You should match a scanner to your needs, whether for print or Web. For example, scanning resolutions can vary greatly, and for print output, you would need a high resolution.

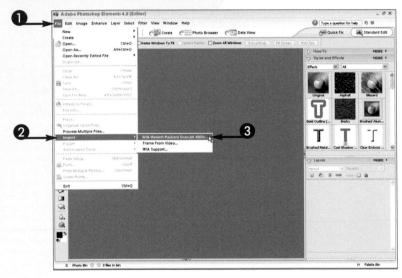

① Click File.

② Click Import.

③ Click a scanner option in the submenu.

Elements searches for scanners at startup. If your scanner is not listed, you should restart Elements or check your scanner settings.

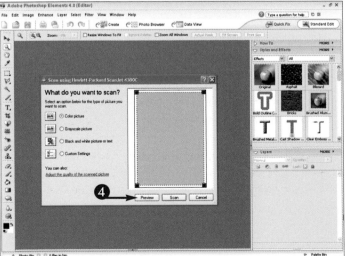

Elements opens your scanner software.

This example uses the Hewlett-Packard ScanJet 4300c.

④ Click the Preview option.

Some scanners use Overview instead of Preview.

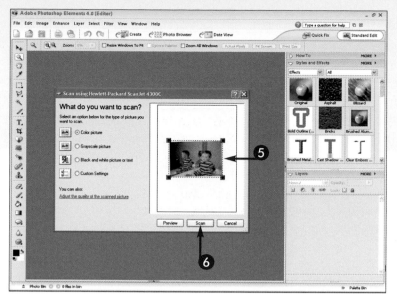

⑤ Click and drag to adjust the selection box to the size and position you want.

⑥ Click Scan.

The scanning program scans the image and imports the scan into Elements.

You may have to close the scanning program, depending on the manufacturer.

Your image appears in a new document.

Did You Know?

Most scanning software offers image adjustment options that you can use before you scan the image. Be cautious when using these adjustments, because after you scan, the changes are permanent. You can perform many more adjustments in Elements with the Undo History tool for error correction.

Put It Together!

You can save a lot of time by placing multiple photos on the scanner, and scanning them all at the same time. Use your selection tools to select an image. Click Layer, then click New, and then click Layer Through Cut, to place the selected image on its own layer. Copy and paste the image layer into a new file and then save the file.

Locate
ONLINE RESOURCES
for Elements 4

You can learn to do new and exciting things in Photoshop Elements by reading books such as this, and by experimenting on your own with your graphics and photos. However, if you want to learn to be even more creative with your graphics work, you can look for Adobe resources on the Internet, many of which cater directly to Photoshop Elements.

You can never learn too many tips from tutorials. There is always a new way to do an old trick, or a brand-new effect that you can learn to apply to your

own work. You can take advantage of many tutorials and tips that you find on the Web to increase your skills with Elements. Experimentation is often the best way to learn how a tool works, and following a tutorial can show you methods and techniques that can be great starting points for you to experiment on your own images.

You can also visit other websites that contain additional tutorials and tips to help you to further develop your skills in Photoshop Elements.

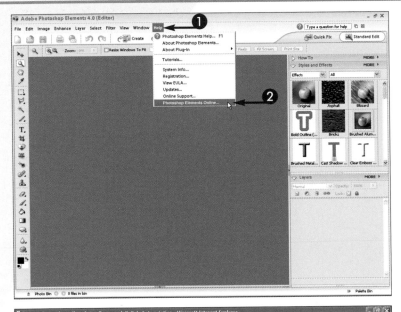

ACCESS THE ADOBE WEBSITE

① Click Help.

② Click Photoshop Elements Online.

The Photoshop Elements website opens in your default Web browser.

③ Click Tutorials.

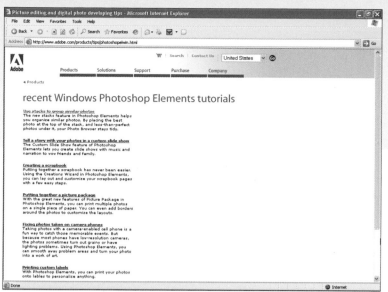

The Photoshop Elements Tutorials page opens.

You can click the links on the page to access step-by-step instructions on how to use Elements.

68

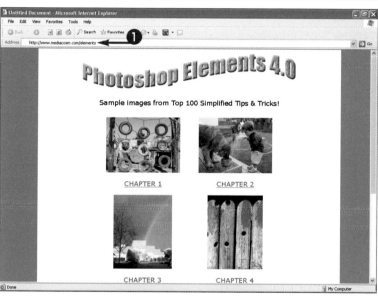

ACCESS EXAMPLES FROM THIS BOOK

① Open your Web browser and type **www.mediacosm.com/elements** in the Address bar.

A website appears with links to sample images from this book that you can use for practice.

Did You Know?

You can find other Photoshop Elements resources on the Internet. There are many websites that dedicate themselves to graphics applications, including Elements. For example, try doing a search for Photoshop Elements Tips on your Internet search engine. Keep in mind that most styles, shapes, and brushes for Photoshop also work in Elements, so you can search for Photoshop resources to build into your Elements tools.

Did You Know?

You can translate Photoshop tutorials into Photoshop Elements tutorials. Many of the steps and filters allow the tutorials to cross over from Photoshop to Elements. By following the steps of a Photoshop tutorial, you can often reproduce the effect, even if it is not specific to Elements.

Organize your palettes with the
PALETTE BIN

Photoshop Elements 4 has a new feature called the Palette Bin. The Palette Bin organizes all of the main palettes into one area on the right side of the workspace. You can also customize it by attaching or detaching any of the available floating palettes. The default layout settings include the How To, Styles and Effects, and Layers palettes. You can also reset to the default settings.

You can add or remove palettes by dragging them on or off the Palette Bin area. When you add palettes, Elements automatically sizes the palette to the set size

of the Bin. You can increase or decrease the width of the Palette Bin, and even hide it completely with a mouse click. You can hide the palette information by collapsing the palette. Collapsing also increases available space for the other palettes in the bin. Each palette also has a drop-down menu that provides additional options.

With the Palette Bin, all of your palette tools are available in one place, and fully customizable for whatever type of project you are working on.

ADD A PALETTE TO THE PALETTE BIN

① Click the More menu in an undocked palette.

② Click Place in Palette Bin when Closed.

③ Click the Close button.

● Elements docks the palette in the Palette Bin.

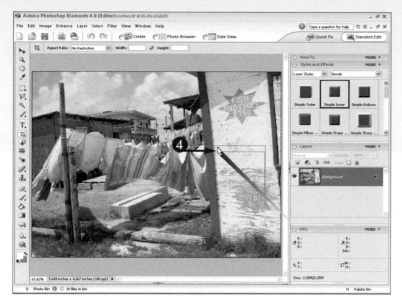

④ Click and drag a palette
from the Palette Bin.

⑤ Release the mouse
button.

DIFFICULTY LEVEL

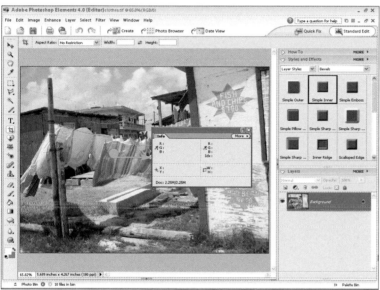

● Elements removes the palette from the
Palette Bin.

TIPS

Did You Know?

You can open or close any undocked palette
by clicking Window and then clicking any
listed palette. Palettes that are already open
are indicated by a small check mark and
should be visible on-screen. If you open or
close a docked palette from the Palette Bin,
this hides or displays the entire Palette Bin,
instead of removing the selected palette.

Did You Know?

You can quickly hide, display, and resize the
Palette Bin by clicking on or dragging the
leftmost edge of the Palette Bin. Your icon
becomes a double line and arrow (◄‖►)
when the cursor is positioned properly to
resize or hide. Click Window, and then click
Reset Palette Locations to return the Palette
Bin to its default settings.

Manage your images with the
PHOTO BIN

You can easily keep track of your open images and quickly select between them by using the new Photo Bin feature. Located at the bottom of the workspace, the Photo Bin allows you to see all available and open images. You can easily switch from one image to another by clicking the different images, which can speed up your workflow when you work on large, complex projects.

The Elements Photo Bin is very versatile, allowing you to sort, group, and rearrange the images within the Photo Bin area. By clicking and dragging images into the Photo Bin, you can sort the images in whatever order you want, so that you can quickly access important images from a large group of images.

You can access other options, such as rotate and duplicate, by right-clicking any image in the Photo Bin. Right-clicking is also a quick way to access the File Info for any image, and allows you to add captions and copyright information, directly from the Photo Bin.

① Open multiple image files in Elements.

● As you open each image, a thumbnail of that image appears in the Photo Bin.

② Click an image that is not visible on-screen.

● Elements displays the image in your workspace.

● You can also click the Previous and Next buttons to rotate between the images in the Photo Bin.

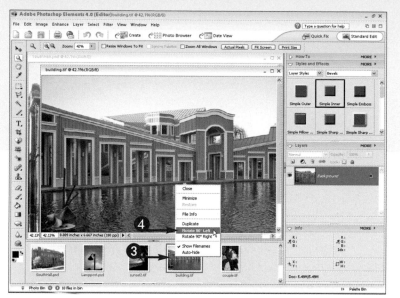

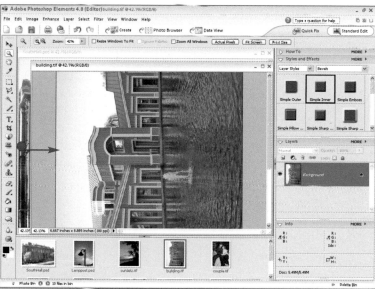

3 Right-click an image.

The Photo Bin image options appear.

4 Select the option you want.

● Elements applies the option.

Did You Know?

You can quickly hide, display, and resize the Photo Bin by clicking or dragging the topmost edge of the palette. Your icon becomes a double line and arrow (◄╫►) when the cursor is in the appropriate place. You can also use the Photo Bin button, located under the lower-left side of the Photo Bin, to open and close the Photo Bin with a single mouse click.

Did You Know?

If you have enough pictures, a scroll bar appears in the Photo Bin area, so you can scroll up and down the rows of images. If you hide the Palette Bin, the Photo Bin automatically extends into the available space, providing additional space for you to view more images across a row.

Organizing Your Photos

Photoshop Elements 4 has a whole new way to organize your photos and images. Elements now incorporates all of the photo organization and creation features from Adobe Album in its new Organizer features. Organizer is a separate application that is closely linked with Elements and that allows you to find, sort, tag, and catalog all of your digital photos from your computer, CD-ROM photo archives, and digital camera.

Organization is generally an arduous task for the digital photographer. However, you can use Organizer to categorize, label, and tag your images for fast sorting to find a photo, to group pictures together by themes, and to add custom information to the metadata of any image.

Organizer has many useful tools and features to help you keep organized. Catalogs look up and store information about every imported image, including thumbnails for visual scanning. Tags allow you to assign custom keywords to similar photos for quick filtering. Collections allow you to group together images that may not have a common thread as with tags, but that you still want to link together. You can also view the cataloged images by filename, file location, and date. You can even keep track of changes to files and folders to keep them up to date.

It may initially take a while to organize all of your images. However, in the long run, Organizer saves you a lot of time by helping you to sort and search more quickly and easily for any image in your collection.

Top 100

Create a new
PHOTO CATALOG

Organizer uses catalogs as the foundation for tracking your image files. Catalogs are the basic information index that Organizer creates from your digital photos, incorporating file information such as location, name, and metadata. You can import individual images as well as entire folders of images; you can even scan your entire computer or a selected hard drive, and Organizer automatically searches out every image.

Organizer recognizes common file formats such as JPEG, TIFF, GIF, and BMP, as well as Adobe PSD and EPS files. It also recognizes common video formats

such as MPEG, AVI, and MOV. Organizer treats video files like image files, importing all of the available data into the Catalog.

Organizer creates a default catalog called My Catalog.psa for your images. Most people only need one catalog for all of their images, but other catalogs can be useful for selected groups of photos or special projects. You can create a new catalog and import any or all of your existing photos, without affecting any other catalogs that you have. This is an excellent tool for professional photographers who work on large-scale projects.

① Click File.

② Click Catalog.

The Catalog dialog box appears.

③ Click New.

● You can import free music into your new catalogs by selecting this option.

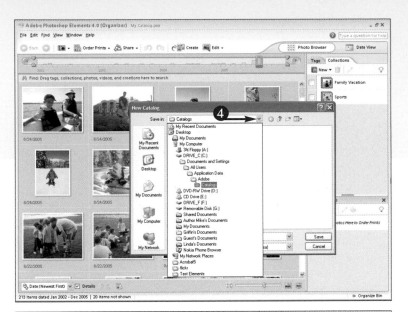

The New Catalog
dialog box appears.

④ Click here and select
the location where you
want to save the file.

By default, catalogs are
saved in C:\Documents
and Settings\All Users\
Application Data\
Adobe\Catalogs.

DIFFICULTY LEVEL

⑤ Type a name for the new catalog.

⑥ Click Save.

Organizer creates and opens a new,
empty catalog.

TIPS

Did You Know?

You cannot delete catalogs directly
from Organizer. In Windows, navigate to
the file folder where the catalog is located
and manually delete it. By default, all
new catalogs are saved in C:\Documents
and Settings\All Users\Application
Data\Adobe\Catalogs, although you can
save your catalogs in any location.

Customize It!

You can import audio file formats such as
MP3 and WAV into your catalog to use as
background music files for Creations. To
be able to import audio files, click View
and then click Media Types. In the Media
Types dialog box that appears, click Audio
to enable importing audio files into a
catalog. Audio files are now included
when you import new files. For more
information, see Chapter 9.

IMPORT IMAGES
into your photo
CATALOG

You can easily import images into your Photo catalog to begin organizing and indexing. Organizer has multiple ways for you to import new images into an existing catalog, from individual files to entire computer searches for any recognized image file formats. Sometimes when you first set up a catalog, it may take a few minutes to find and import all of the files, but it is worth the wait.

You can locate and import files with Organizer in minutes, a task that would otherwise take weeks to do manually. You can then visually scan and delete any undesired images from the catalog. When selecting a folder of images, you can choose to import from all subfolders within that folder as well, or exclude them.

You can also import images from outside the computer. For example, Organizer can import images from digital cameras, scanners, and even palm pilots and cell phones. Simply connect them to the computer and select the appropriate source from the menu.

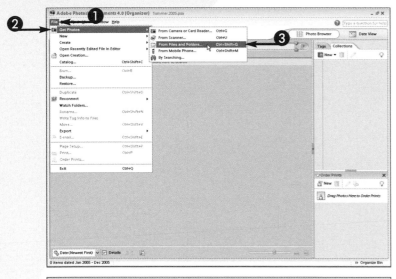

❶ Click File.

❷ Click Get Photos.

❸ Click From Files and Folders.

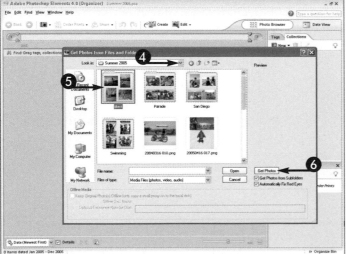

The Get Photos from Files and Folders dialog box appears.

❹ Click here and select the source file or folder.

❺ Click the file or folder you want.

❻ Click Get Photos.

Organizer displays the newly imported files.

● If duplicate files are found, a dialog box appears to list these files for review.

TIPS

Caution!

When you search the entire hard drive on your computer, Organizer does not recognize the difference between images that you want and images that you do not want. For example, Web banners, splash screens, and Internet cache images are all included when you search the whole computer. You may want to be specific when selecting folder locations from which you want to import. This reduces the amount of unwanted images to a manageable level.

Did You Know?

You can import additional images into the catalog at any time by clicking File and then clicking Import. In the Import dialog box, select your source while you have your destination catalog open in Organizer. The images automatically import into the open catalog.

CATEGORIZE
your images

You can use categories to begin your sorting process. Categories are general descriptions that specify a basic idea or group that you want as an identifier for your images.

Organizer has already set up several default categories such as People, Places, Events, and Other. Each of these categories can contain many different specific subgroups, but at the same time cover some of the basic areas common to photos. You can create and customize completely new categories and subcategories to divide up one very broad descriptor

like Places into more detailed categories such as your home, a specific state or country, or even a street or building.

Categories are easy to make and assign to an image or group of images. You can assign more than one category or subcategory to a single image to allow for multiple descriptors. For example, assigning multiple categories to a single image allows for the image to be included in each of the categories when sorting by individual categories. This is a great benefit when you have images that contain multiple subjects.

1 In the Tags palette, click New.

2 Click New Category.

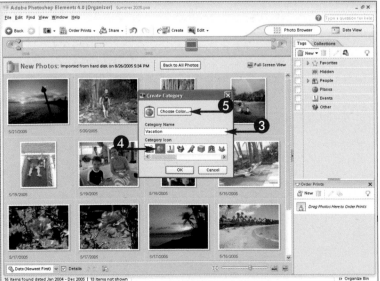

The Create Category dialog box appears.

3 Type a name for the new category.

4 Click a Category Icon button to choose an icon.

Organizer assigns the icon.

5 Click Choose Color.

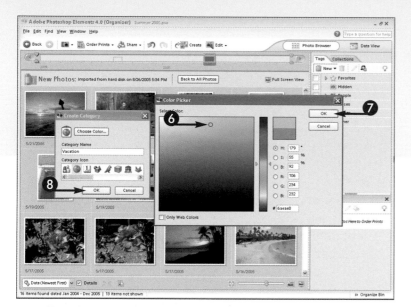

The Color Picker dialog box appears.

⑥ Click the color you want.

⑦ Click OK to close the Color Picker dialog box.

⑧ Click OK to close the Create Category dialog box.

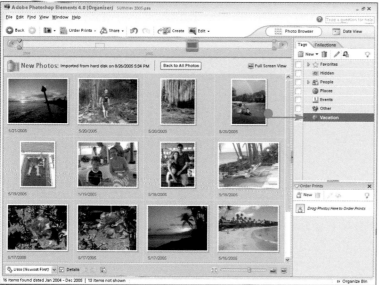

Organizer creates the new category.

● Tags created in the category will have the color you selected.

TIPS

Did You Know?
By right-clicking a category in the Tags palette, you can edit the category — allowing you to change the name, icon, and color — or delete the category. Right-clicking also allows you to create a new category, subcategory, or tag.

Caution!
When you delete a category or subcategory, you are also deleting all subcategories and tags contained within the deleted selection. By doing so, you also delete all tags and subcategories assigned to your catalog images. Be sure that you are not accidentally deleting a subcategory or tag that you want to keep. You can use the Undo feature to reverse an immediate deletion, but after Organizer is closed, the data is lost.

Create a new
KEY TAG

Key tags are an integral part to indexing in Organizer. Key tags assign specific sorting or filtering data to an image, including options for a custom icon and custom text that accurately describes the theme for the tag. Using key tags, you can quickly and easily sort and find your images whenever you need them.

Tags can be found under any category or subcategory, and typically describe a more specific instance within the main category or subcategory.

In the Tags palette, key tags are the lowest level in the hierarchy, being assigned to a given category or subcategory with no additional levels allowed below a tag.

Because you can customize a key tag, it is important to name the photo subject or content appropriately. Key tags are used for searching, sorting, and filtering images, and so the more descriptive the key tag name, the easier it is to use. For more information about searching with key tags, see Task #77.

① In the Tags palette, click New.

② Click New Tag.

The Create Tag dialog box appears.

③ Click here and select a category for the new tag.

④ Type a name and descriptive text for the tag.

⑤ Click Edit Icon.

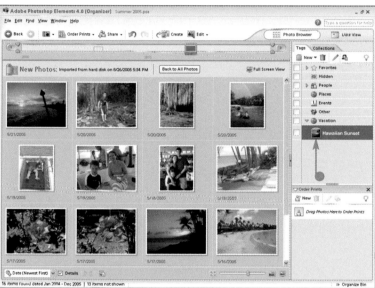

The Edit Tag Icon dialog box appears.

6 Click Import.

The Import Image for Tag Icon window appears.

7 Click here and select the image file you want.

8 Click Open.

9 Click OK to close the Edit Tag Icon dialog box.

10 Click OK to close the Create Tag dialog box.

● Elements creates the new tag.

#74

DIFFICULTY LEVEL

TIPS

Did You Know?

You can convert a key tag into a category. This is useful when a key tag has enough images that you want to divide them into separate, unique groups related by a common topic. Right-click a key tag and select Change tag to subcategory from the pop-up menu. All images assigned to that key tag remain in the new subcategory, and you can assign new key tags to individual images.

Did You Know?

You can also convert a subcategory into a tag. Right-click a subcategory and click Change subcategory to a tag from the pop-up menu. This changes the subcategory into a new key tag in which you can add notes or assign an image that represents the key tag subject as an icon.

ASSIGN TAGS
to images

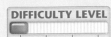

You can use tags to assign specific and detailed descriptions to your images. Tags are similar to categories for grouping related images together, but you can use tags to divide categories into defined groups for more specific sorting. For example, you can have a category for Travel, and assign tags for specific locations to which you have traveled.

As you assign each tag, an icon appears below the image thumbnail in the Photo Bin, representing the key tag. You can assign as many tags as you like to an image, but if you have too many key tags assigned to an image, you may consider revising your tags to prevent confusion.

DIFFICULTY LEVEL

When you edit a name, icon, or category location in the Tag palette, all of the associated images update. You can also delete tags from an image when the tags are no longer useful, or delete a tag from the Tag palette altogether. Deleting a tag removes it from all images to which it was assigned.

❶ Select the files to which you want to assign a tag.

You can Ctrl+click to select multiple, separate files.

❷ Click and drag the tag you want onto the selected files.

❸ Release the mouse button.

Organizer assigns the tag to all of the images you selected.

TAGS TO FACES

DIFFICULTY LEVEL

You can use Elements' face-recognition feature to find the faces in your photos and display them for easy tagging. Elements automatically scans photos in Organizer for the colors and physical structures that are characteristic of human faces. To access the feature, click the Find Faces for Tagging icon in the Tags palette.

The Face Tagging dialog box that appears gives you access to all of your Organizer tags. You can create custom tags in the People category for the friends and family members whose faces often

appear in your photos. To apply tags, you click and drag them to the faces, the same way you apply tags to regular photos. To apply the same tag to multiple faces, control-click the faces in the Face Tagging dialog box before applying the tag.

Multiple faces that appear in same photo will show up as separate faces in the Face Tagging dialog box. When you select a face, the original photo appears in the bottom-right corner of the dialog box.

① Click the Tags palette.

② Click the Find Faces for Tagging icon.

Elements searches for the faces in your photos and displays those faces in the Face Tagging dialog box.

③ Click a face.

④ Click a tag and drag it to the face.

Elements applies the tag and hides the face in the dialog box.

● You can click Show Already Tagged Faces to display it again.

⑤ Click Done to close the dialog box.

Search your photos with the
FIND MENU

You can use the Find menu to locate a particular image or range of images that do not have an assigned key tag, or that may contain many different tags within the group. The Find menu enables you to save time that you would normally spend scrolling or manually searching for your images, and quickly filters out unwanted categories and key tags.

The Find Menu in Organizer has nine different methods to filter out your images to reveal only the ones you want, based on the conditions that you set from the menu choices. For example, you can sort by

filename, date, and captions. Some menu items have submenus, such as History, where you can base your search on the movement and exchange history of the image.

You can use multiple conditions to locate your images. For example, you can assign a range of dates to search, and then specify another Find condition, such as search by filename, to those results. Elements returns only images with your selected Find menu condition, within the range of dates that you specified.

FIND BY FILENAME

① Click Find.

② Click By Filename.

The Find by Filename dialog box appears.

③ Type the text for the search.

④ Click OK.

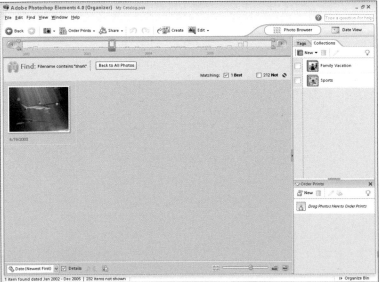

Organizer filters for the matching files.

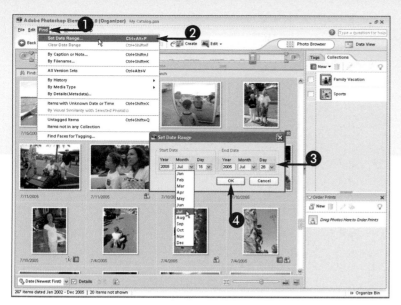

FIND BY DATE RANGE

① Click Find.

② Click Set Date Range.

The Set Date Range dialog box appears.

③ Select the dates for the search.

④ Click OK.

DIFFICULTY LEVEL

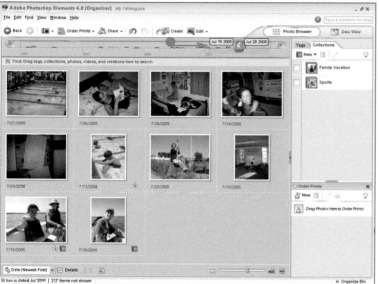

Organizer filters for the date range.

● The margins for the range of dates change to match the dates you selected.

TIPS

Customize It!

When you apply a Find menu command, several additional filter options appear in the Find area. For example, you can select the Best option (☐ changes to ☑) to show images that meet the Find condition. You can also select the Not option (☐ changes to ☑) to view images that do not meet the Find condition. If you select both options, then all of the images appear.

Customize It!

You can also use the sliders in the Date Range area to specify a date range. Simply move the left and right sliders into the positions that you want. Organizer automatically restricts images in the Photo Well to the dates between the slider positions.

Identify
FAVORITES AND HIDDEN
images

You can use two special tags to organize and clean up your Photo Well. Unlike other tags, the Favorites and Hidden tags have special properties that prohibit their renaming and deletion. Favorites and Hidden tags allow you to drag and drop an assignment to an image and conduct a search based on this assignment.

The Favorites tag is similar to a category, and contains several subcategories for ranking images; these subcategories are also not editable. The Favorites tag is useful for selecting specific images out of a similar group. For example, you can tag certain images from an event with this category to separate them from the rest of the images.

When you assign the Hidden tag to an image in a particular category, the image does not appear in the Photo Well. It remains in the catalog, but is hidden from view, so that your Photo Well remains less cluttered with images. Instead of deleting images from the catalog, you can still have the hidden images available for a future project, but they do not take up viewing space.

IDENTIFY USING THE FAVORITES TAG

① Select the images you want to tag.

② Click and drag the Favorites tag onto one of the selected images.

Organizer assigns the Favorites tag to all of the selected images.

③ Click the box to the left of the Favorites tag.

Organizer only displays images with the Favorites tag in the Photo Well.

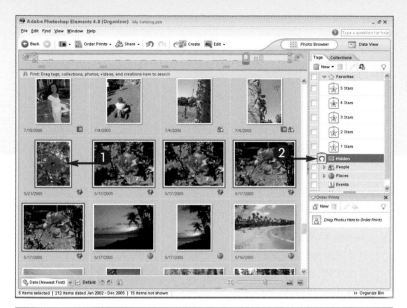

① Select the images you want to tag.

② Click and drag the Hidden tag onto one of the selected images.

Organizer assigns the Hidden tag to all of the selected images.

The next time you view the catalog, the images you assigned with the Hidden tag will not appear in the Photo Well.

● You can click the box to the left of the Hidden tag to only display images with the Hidden tag in the Photo Well.

TIPS

Did You Know?

If you use the Hidden tag as a search criterion, then any images with the Hidden tag appear in the Photo Well. This is useful for finding all images with a certain tag, including those that are hidden. If you find a file in the Hidden group that you like, you can remove the Hidden tag so that the image once again displays in the Photo Well.

Did You Know?

You can use one Favorites tag at a time on any image. This means that you cannot place a five-star Favorites tag on an image and a three-star Favorites tag on the same image. When you apply a Favorites tag, it replaces any previous Favorites tag. No other tags are affected by this restriction.

Create a
COLLECTION

You can use an organizational tool called a collection to group multiple images together under the same descriptive name. However, instead of grouping images with a specific subject or theme, you can create groups of images that share a specific use or project. You can also create groups to organize collections with related themes or ideas.

Collections now support hierarchy, meaning that you can divide them into collection groups and collections of images. You cannot assign images directly to a collection group. Instead, you must assign images to

a collection, and place the collection into a collection group. If you search by collection, the Photo Well is restricted to the contents of only one collection.

You can rearrange the photo order in collections. In the Photo Well, you cannot move or change the order of images, but in the Collection palette, when you search by your collection, you can move them into whatever order you want. Organizer automatically numbers them in sequence for you, making it easy to customize a series.

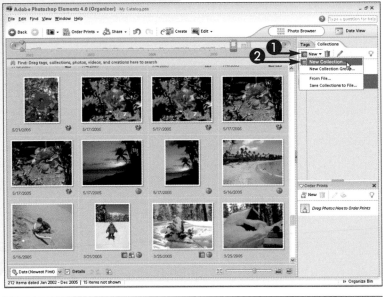

❶ Click New.

❷ Click New Collection.

The Create Collection dialog box appears.

❸ Click here and select a Group.

❹ Type a name and descriptive text for the collection.

❺ Click Edit Icon.

170

The Edit Collection Icon dialog box appears.

6 Click Import.

The Import Image for Collection Icon window appears.

7 Click here and select the image file you want.

8 Click Open.

9 Click OK to close the Edit Collection Icon dialog box.

10 Click OK to close the Create Collection dialog box.

Elements creates the new collection.

11 Click the box next to the new category.

Elements displays the empty collection.

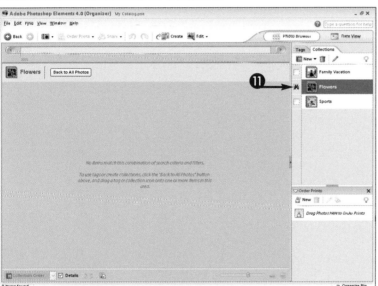

Customize It!

To quickly make a Creation with a collection, you can press Ctrl+A to select all of the images in the collection, and then click the Creation button. All of the selected images appear in the Creation that you choose. Collections allow you to work on Creations without reselecting the original images every time you open Organizer. You can learn more about Creations in Chapter 9.

Did You Know?

You can quickly assign an image to a collection. Right-click any image in the Photo Well, click Add To Collection, and then choose from the existing collections in the submenu. You can also assign collections by dragging and dropping the image onto a collection in the Collection palette.

Watch folders for
UPDATES

You can quickly update your image catalog in Organizer by assigning a folder to watch for updates. You can assign folders in a catalog that you want Organizer to check regularly for changes in file content. When you add a new image to a folder, the next time you open Organizer, you can choose to be notified or have Organizer automatically add the images to the catalog.

You can avoid having to import photos that you save to your folders by placing them in a watched folder, and Organizer does the work for you. When

Organizer imports the photos, you can view the files and apply whatever tags or categories you want.

You can tell Organizer to watch any folder on your computer, even if it is not a folder that is imported into your catalog. Organizer adds the images from the folder into the open catalog. For example, you can create a new folder for future images, add it to the watch list, and as you save images to the folder, you also save them to the catalog. This is a great time saver.

① Click File.

② Click Watch Folders.

The Watch Folders dialog box appears.

③ Click Add.

The Browse For Folder dialog box appears.

④ Navigate to the folder you want to watch.

⑤ Click OK.

172

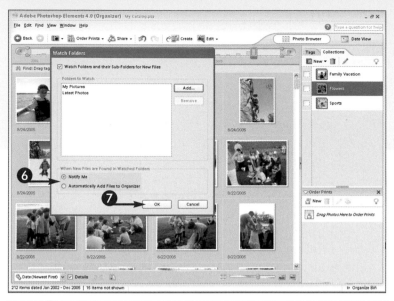

6 Select the When New Files are Found in Watched Folders option (○ changes to ◉).

7 Click OK.

Organizer now monitors the selected folder for changes.

TIPS

Did You Know?

You can also have Organizer watch subfolders. When you select the subfolders option at the top of the Watch Folder dialog box (☐ changes to ☑), Organizer automatically watches the content of the folder you choose, along with its subfolders.

Customize It!

You can easily stop the Watch Folders feature. Open the Watch Folders dialog box, select a folder that is currently being watched, and click the Remove button. Organizer no longer watches that folder or its subfolders.

Caution!

Depending on the number of images within a folder, Organizer may take a while to update. If you have a large number of images in a subfolder, then select that subfolder to apply this feature to it, instead of to the larger, main folder.

Chapter 9

Working with Creations in Organizer

Photoshop Elements 4 has a completely new way to organize your images. This is because it now incorporates all of the photo organization and creation features of Adobe Album. A separate application from Elements, Adobe Album has become a new Organizer feature. Organizer is a separate application that is closely linked with Elements, and that allows you to find, sort, tag, and catalog all of your digital photos from your computer, CD-ROM photo archives, and digital camera.

Organization has always been a difficult task for the digital photographer, whether at home or professionally. You can use the tools in Organizer to categorize, label, and tag your digital images. This allows you to quickly find a photo, group pictures together by common themes, and add custom information to the metadata of an image for future use.

Organizer lets you create and use catalogs to look up and store information about every imported image, including thumbnails for visual scanning. Tags allow you to assign custom keywords to similar photos so that you can quickly filter a group of photos to show only certain images. Collections allow you to group together images even when they do not have a common thread. You can view your cataloged images in different ways, including by filename, file location, and date. You can even track changes to files and folders to keep them up to date.

You will save time by organizing all of your files. Whether you are searching for a specific image or a group of related images, Organizer speeds up your search so that you can spend more time working with your files.

Top 100

Select and set up a
CREATION TYPE

Photoshop Organizer has many great creations from which you can choose. The quickest way to start a new creation is through the Create button feature in the menu bar area. With one click, you can choose from any of the seven main creation types.

When you click the Create button, the Creation Setup splash screen appears, displaying the seven creation types. When you click a creation type, the splash graphic changes, and gives you a brief description of what the creation does.

Many creations use similar starting steps. For example, they all allow you to choose a creation layout template, and to select the images you want to use for the creation. When you learn how to do these steps in one task, you can apply them to other creations. You should experiment with the different creations so that you become familiar with the processes for each of them. The task below is referenced by several other tasks in this book to avoid unnecessary repetition.

① Click Photo Browser to open Organizer.

② Click Create.

The Creation Setup splash screen appears.

③ Click a creation type.

④ Click OK.

The Creation Set-up window appears.

Note: *Some Setup windows may vary from the example. Slideshows and VCD with Menu screens will progress differently.*

5 Click the template style you want.

6 Click Next Step.

7 Click Add Photos.

The Add Photos dialog box appears.

8 Click the check box next to the images you want to use (☐ changes to ☑).

9 Click Done.

10 Click Next Step at the bottom of each screen to complete the process.

TIPS

Did You Know?

You can speed up your creation design by preselecting your images before you click the Create button. When you reach the Arrange Your Photos window in the creation process, your preselected images appear automatically in the photo area. You can also use images from a collection in the same way. When you select the collection you want and click the Create button, your collection images appear in the Arrange Your Photos window.

Customize It!

When you click a creation type in the Creation Setup, Organizer displays the types of media that are available for that creation type. These media types are represented by icons, and include printing to a PDF file, using VCD format, viewing on a computer, and sharing through e-mail. Check to see which media options are available for the creation types that interest you.

Create a
CONTACT SHEET of photos

You can easily create a contact sheet of your favorite photographs in Organizer. A contact sheet contains a selection of smaller versions of your original images. This excellent feature allows you to quickly print out and preview your images without having to go through the expense of printing them at full size.

You can customize your contact sheets by specifying the number of columns of images you want to appear on each page. You can specify up to nine columns of thumbnails, and Organizer automatically scales the

thumbnails to fit the page. You can specify a maximum of 81 images for each contact sheet, based on nine columns. You can also choose from different labeling options, such as filename and date.

You can pre-select your images before you print your contact sheets. You can also import additional images from within the Print dialog box. When you import images from within the Print dialog box, you can select images based on tag name or category, or you can print out the entire catalog.

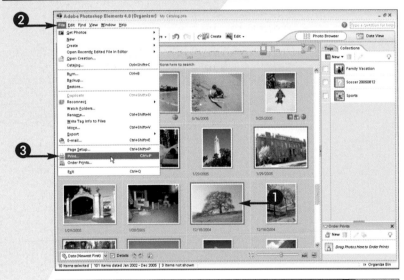

① Click the image or images you want to print.

② Click File.

③ Click Print.

The Print Selected Photos dialog box appears.

④ Click here and select Contact Sheet.

⑤ Click here to select the number of columns you want.

● You can click to select the Text Label options you want (☐ changes to ☑).

⑥ Click Add to add more photos to your contact sheets.

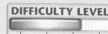

The Add Photos dialog box appears.

⑦ Click the check box next to the images you want (☐ changes to ☑).

● You can click an Add Photos From option to find groups of images (○ changes to ◉).

⑧ Click Done.

● Organizer adds the images you selected to your contact sheets.

● You can remove images by clicking them in the left column and then clicking the Minus icon.

● You can move among multiple contact sheets by clicking the directional arrows (◀ and ▶).

⑨ Click Print.

Organizer prints your contact sheets.

DIFFICULTY LEVEL

TIPS

Caution!

You can lose image detail when you select too many columns for your contact sheets, so consider how you intend to use them. For example, if you use them for a client or customer, then you can keep the column number lower for larger thumbnails that have more detail. For some archives, you may prefer smaller images, to reduce the total number of printable pages that you generate.

Did You Know?

You can output your contact sheets to different formats. For example, you can save them as Microsoft Office document images, or as PDF files. These methods allow you to save a file to your system for future use, without having to print it.

Design a
PICTURE PACKAGE

You can select an image or images that you want to print and then use Organizer to generate picture packages. Picture packages are a great tool for both professional and home users, which allow you to select multiple sizes of a single image for a variety of framing and printing purposes. You can even group multiple images together into a single picture package, so you can create a variety of images on a single page template, instead of multiple pages of one image each.

Organizer's picture package tool has 15 predesigned layout templates that contain the most commonly

used photo sizes in different configurations. You can apply 24 custom frames to the images from the picture package layout. You can combine the custom frames and layout templates to make your photographs look more interesting.

You can also change the order of your images in the picture package. To do this, you can simply drag them into different arrangements on the current page. This is useful when you import images from multiple locations.

① Click the image or images you want to print.

② Click File.

③ Click Print.

The Print Selected Photos dialog box appears.

④ Click here and select Picture Package.

⑤ Click the arrows to select the layout and frame options you want.

● You can click here to fill the page with the first photo selected (☐ changes to ☑).

⑥ Click Add to add more photos to your picture package.

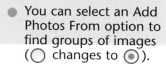

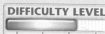
The Add Photos dialog box appears.

⑦ Click the check box next to the images you want to add (☐ changes to ☑).

● You can select an Add Photos From option to find groups of images (○ changes to ◉).

⑧ Click Done.

Organizer adds the images you selected to the picture package.

● You can remove images by clicking them in the left column and then clicking the Minus icon.

● You can move among multiple pages by clicking the directional arrows (◀ and ▶).

⑨ Click Print.

Organizer prints the images.

TIPS

Did You Know?

Picture packages are a great way to reprint old photos that you have restored in Elements. Create a picture package with these restored images by using standard photo-sized template styles. Then print the images on high-quality photo paper. The result is a brand-new photograph from an old print. This is a wonderful way to share family photos from old photo albums.

Caution!

You can add or subtract images any time before you print. However, adding or removing an image from your selected photos will cause the picture package layouts to reset to the original image order. Be sure to add and remove the images you want before you rearrange your images in order to avoid unnecessarily resetting your photo order.

Construct a
PHOTO GALLERY for the Web

You can use Organizer to create a photo gallery website that displays your digital images. In addition to sizing and optimizing your image files for the website, Organizer also creates the Web pages that display the images and then links those pages together.

In the photo gallery, a miniature image, or thumbnail, represents each gallery image. You can click the thumbnail to view the image at its regular size. The photo gallery also contains buttons that

allow you to navigate between the different pages that display the thumbnails.

The photo gallery feature is useful if you want a quick and easy way to build a website for your digital photos, but do not want to create the HTML pages manually. After you create your photo gallery, you can use a Web publishing program such as Macromedia Dreamweaver or Adobe GoLive to upload all of the image and HTML files to a Web server. You can also use an FTP program to transfer the files.

① Click File.

② Click Create.

③ Click HTML Photo Gallery.

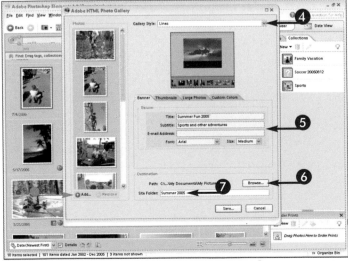

The Adobe HTML Photo Gallery dialog box appears.

● You can click Add to add photos or Remove to remove photos.

④ Click here and select the Web template you want from the Gallery Style menu.

⑤ Type your banner information and choose formatting options here.

⑥ Click Browse and specify where to put the gallery folder.

⑦ Type the name of the gallery folder.

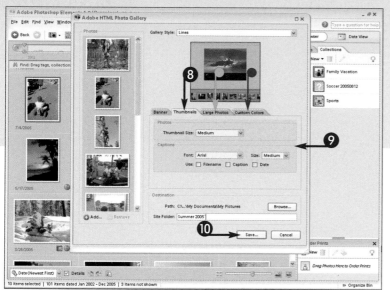

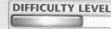

8 Click the Thumbnails tab.

9 Select the caption preferences for the Web gallery thumbnail images.

● You can click the Large Photos tab to specify preferences for the larger images and captions.

● You can click the Custom Colors tab to specify the website colors.

10 Click Save.

Organizer creates the HTML Photo Gallery files and saves them to the gallery folder.

A gallery preview appears in a Web browser window.

TIPS

Customize It!

Even after you set the other preferences, you can still customize your photo gallery Web pages by selecting different gallery styles. The different styles add themes to your gallery and display the images in different arrangements. Some of the themes include office, outer space, and theater. When you select a gallery style, Organizer automatically applies the new theme without altering the other settings.

Did You Know?

You can further customize your photo gallery Web pages by opening and editing the HTML pages with a Web publishing program or HTML editor. This enables you to change titles, text styles, colors, and other features on the Web pages that you cannot customize in Organizer.

Create a
SLIDE SHOW

The slide show feature in Organizer helps you easily share image collections with family, friends, and coworkers. During the creation process, you specify a set of photos, the slide duration, transitions between, and other settings, and then save as a project in Organizer.

Organizer also offers a wide variety of transition selections, such as Fade, Blinds, and Spiral, that enable the slide show to move smoothly from slide to slide. In the Slide Show Editor, you can add special effects to your slide show in the form of cartoon clip

art or fancy lettering. A narration feature allows you to add commentary to each slide using your computer's microphone. You can also add panning and zooming effects to your slides, which will scan across a slide as it displays or focus in on a specific detail.

Exporting to the WMV or PDF format makes it easy to share your pictures with others. People can view WMV files using Windows Media Player and PDF files using Adobe Acrobat Reader.

① Click Create.

The Creation Setup window opens.

② Click Slide Show.

③ Click OK.

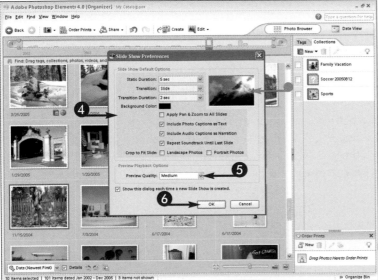

The Slide Show Preferences window appears.

④ Specify the duration, transition, and other options.

● You can click the thumbnail image to see an example of the selected transition.

⑤ Click here to specify the preview quality.

⑥ Click OK.

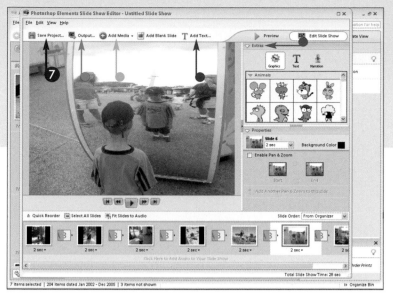

The Slide Show Editor appears.

● You can click Add Media to add more slides to your project.

● You can click Add Text to overlay text on your slides.

● The Extras palette lets you add clip art, fancy text, or narration.

● You can click Output to save the slide show as a separate WMV or PDF file.

⑦ Click Save Project.

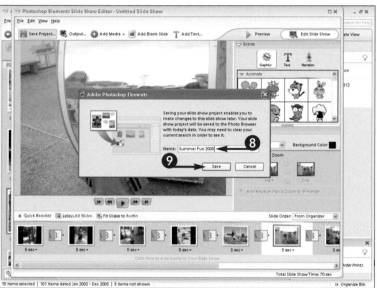

The Adobe Photoshop Elements dialog box appears.

⑧ Type a name for your slide show.

⑨ Click Save.

Organizer saves the slide show.

The new slide show appears at the top of Organizer.

TIPS

Did You Know?
You can rearrange slides in your project in the Slide Show Editor dialog box. Click and drag the photo thumbnails at the bottom to change their order. To remove a slide entirely, right-click it and click Delete Slide.

Caution!
Try to avoid making slide shows that are too large. Each image or sound file that you add to the slide show increases the total file size. Try to limit the size of your sound and image files, so that others can easily download and view your slide show.

Create a
VCD WITH MENU

You can use Organizer to create custom DVDs of your image slide shows to share with friends and family. You can also compile your custom slide shows and arrange them in VCD, or video CD, format that plays in any standard DVD player or DVD-ROM drive.

The VCD can only use movie or video formats. You can use Organizer's slide show export feature to save your slide show into WMV format files that you can burn to CD-ROM. The VCD format uses the filenames

of your slide shows to generate a menu of options. You should therefore use clearly descriptive filenames in your slide shows to make the VCD easier to navigate and use.

You can easily add any WMV files you want to your VCD. When you import the files into your catalog, you can simply select the ones you want to appear on your custom VCD.

1 Click File.

2 Click Create.

3 Click VCD with Menu.

The Create a VCD with Menu dialog box appears.

● You can click Add Slide Shows or Remove Slide Show to arrange slide shows in your VCD.

4 Click a video option based on where the slide show will be viewed (◯ changes to ◉).

5 Click Burn.

● Organizer converts the slide show to .WMV movie file format for burning.

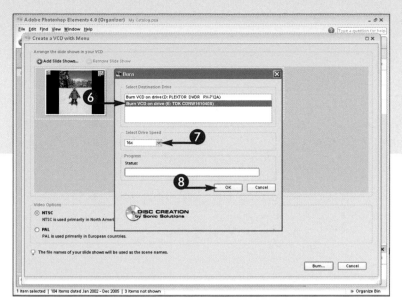

The Burn dialog box appears.

6 Select the destination drive.

7 Click here and select the drive speed.

8 Click OK.

86

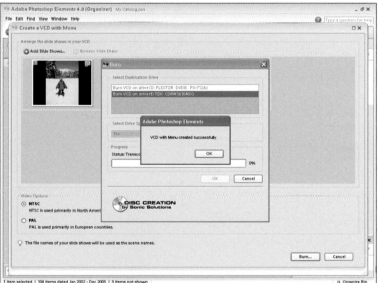

Organizer compiles and generates the VCD.

TIPS

Caution!

When you use Organizer's Create a VCD feature, you can only burn to VCD slide shows that you export as WMV files. The VCD feature does not work with PDF-based slide shows.

Did You Know?

When you create custom slide shows, it is very easy to end up with large file sizes. If you intend to create a VCD, then you may want to create several small slide shows instead of a few large slide shows. This speeds up the process of generating the slide shows, and provides more menu content for your VCD.

Design photo
ALBUM PAGES

You can use Organizer to design attractive scrapbook pages and photo albums without the mess and hassle of scissors and glue. Organizer's creation feature allows you to create custom photo-album pages that you can print out and include in your scrapbook. This creation feature enables you to import photos from your catalog and arrange them in the order you want them to appear. You can then add custom captions, headers, and footers to each photo album page.

Organizer has 19 layout templates that you can choose from to enhance your photo album pages.

When you import your images, you can customize how many images you want to appear on each page, up to a maximum of four. You can also specify a pattern for the number of images you want to appear on each page, for example, one on the first, three on the second, and two on the last. Organizer repeats the pattern until it has used all of the images.

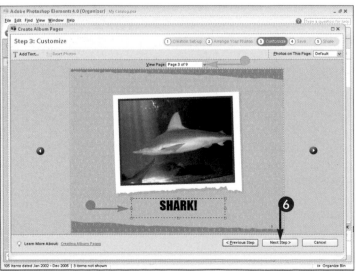

① Set up a photo album creation by selecting Photo Album Pages from the Creation Set-up window.

Note: For more information, see Task #81.

② In the Customize window, click Add Text.

A custom text box appears.

③ Type and format your text.

④ Click Done.

Elements adds the text to the page.

⑤ Click here to advance to the next album page.

● You can double-click a caption text box to insert or edit a caption.

● You can click here to switch to any available view page.

⑥ When you finish editing the captions, click Next Step.

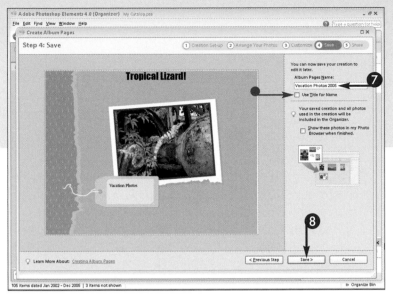

The Save window appears.

⑦ Type a name for the photo album creation.

● Click this check box to use the photo album title for the filename (☐ changes to ☑).

⑧ Click Save.

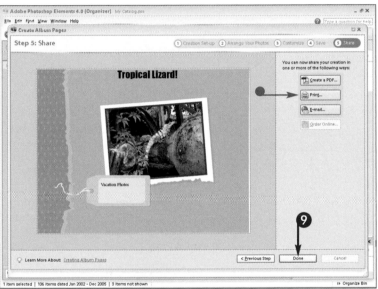

The Share window appears.

● You can select one of several ways in which to share the photo album.

⑨ Click Done.

TIPS

Customize It!
You can accent your album pages with a range of font and text options for your captions, headers, footers, and custom text. You can use any available font style in Elements and Organizer, including boldface, italic, and text color. You can even change the direction of the text from horizontal to vertical.

Caution!
Because you often print your photo albums and scrapbook pages, you should use high-quality images when you design your creations. Low-quality images may appear grainy or may have poor detail in print.

Create a
CARD for special occasions

You can design four-fold custom greeting cards in Organizer for any occasion. With the card creation feature in Organizer, you can use any image from your catalog as the front face of your card. You can also customize the text on the front and inside of the card, to design a special card for your family and friends.

Organizer offers 46 card layout templates that enable you to create a custom card, such as for a birthday or wedding. These templates provide the basic

layouts for the card that you can customize with your own images and text.

You can alter the photographs by resizing them to change the viewable portion of the image. The frame crops your photo to show the part of the photo you want visible. When you scale an image, you affect how the viewable portion of the image appears within the confines of the selected frame style. You can use this technique to focus attention on a specific part of an image instead of the entire image.

① Set up a card creation by selecting Card from the Creation Set-up window.

Note: *For more information, see Task #81.*

② Double-click the text box.

A custom text box appears.

③ Type and format your text.

④ Click Done.

⑤ Click the Next Page button.

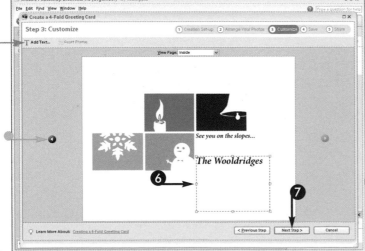

The inside of the card layout appears.

⑥ Double-click here to insert a greeting or message.

● You can click Add Text to create a custom text box.

● You can click here to return to the front of the card.

⑦ Click Next Step.

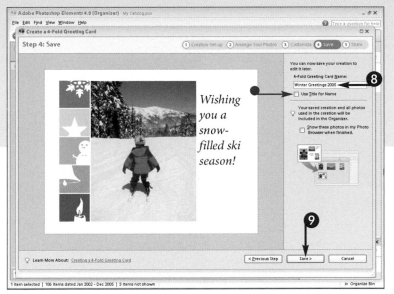

The Save window appears.

8 Type a name for the creation.

● You can click this check box to use the card title for the filename (☐ changes to ☑).

9 Click Save.

The Share window appears.

● You can select one of several ways in which to share the card.

10 Click Done.

Customize It!

You can rearrange the layout of your text boxes when you are creating a card. Click anywhere inside a text box to select it, then click and drag the text box to where you want it to appear on the card. You can also resize and reshape the text box by clicking it to select it, and then using the bounding box anchor points to stretch and shape the text box. This also affects the text layout within the text box.

Caution!

As with many creations available in Organizer, the card creation is intended for print. You should use high-quality, high-resolution pictures, in order to avoid pixelation and loss of detail.

Design a
POSTCARD

You can use your photos to create a postcard that is suitable for mailing. Organizer has a creation feature for designing postcards that you can customize by using any image from your catalog. You can also add titles and messages, and rearrange the card layout. Organizer offers 21 custom layout templates, which use a wide variety of frame designs and color schemes.

You can customize your postcard in several different ways. For example, you can scale or move your image to affect how the image appears within the selected template frame. You can also add custom text boxes for additional messages and effects.

Organizer also offers several ways to share your postcard. For example, you can e-mail it, print it for mailing, or save it as a PDF file for sharing online. You can also save the postcard to your computer so that you can re-open it later in Organizer and make changes. This is a useful way to keep and reuse design styles that you like.

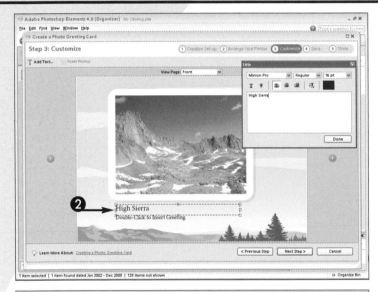

① Set up a postcard creation by selecting Photo Greeting Card from the Creation Set-up window.

Note: *For more information, see Task #81.*

② Double-click the text box and type a card title.

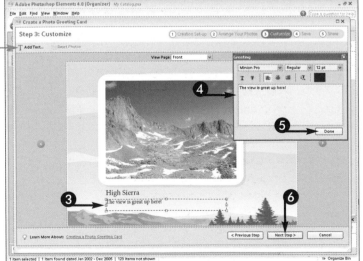

③ Double-click the text box.

A custom text box appears.

④ Type and format your text.

⑤ Click Done.

● You can click Add Text to create a custom text box.

⑥ Click Next Step.

The Save window appears.

⑦ Type a name for the postcard.

● Click this check box to use the postcard title as the filename (☐ changes to ☑).

⑧ Click Save.

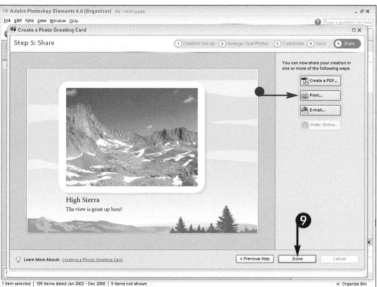

The Share window appears.

● You can select one of several ways in which to share the postcard.

⑨ Click Done.

TIPS

Customize It!

You can move titles, messages, and custom text boxes within the postcard layout. After clicking a text box to select it, you can drag it to a new location on your postcard. You can also change the shape and size of the text box by dragging the bounding box edges.

Customize It!

You should use high-quality, high-resolution images for your postcard creations to ensure good print clarity and to prevent pixelation or poor image quality in your final printout. Also, because you send postcards directly through the mail, you should print on high-quality card stock for durability during mailing.

Create a
PHOTO WALL CALENDAR

You can use the Calendar creation feature in Organizer to design an attractive souvenir photowall calendar for friends and family. Using photos from your catalogs, you can arrange the images in any order, and select a date range of up to five years for the calendar. For example, you can select the years up to 2012.

Each calendar page contains an area in which you can enter a caption that pertains to the photo or the month. You can also customize the appearance of the text by specifying the font, color, and size. In

addition, you can add more text to the page, and apply the same text options as you can with the caption.

Calendars are usually printed. High-resolution images are strongly recommended for clarity. Organizer will prompt you with a warning dialog box about lower than ideal resolution on images, and mark them with a warning symbol. If you are creating calendars for online use only, you can overlook the low-resolution images. Printing these images will result in a very poor quality on paper.

① Click File.

② Click Create.

③ Click Calendar Pages.

The Creation Set-up window appears.

④ Click a calendar template style.

Organizer updates the template preview to the new selection.

⑤ Click here and select a beginning month and year.

⑥ Click here and select an ending month and year.

⑦ Click Next Step.

The Arrange Your Photos window appears.

● You can click here to add, reuse, or remove photos.

⑧ Arrange your images by dragging them into different positions.

Images marked *Not Used* do not appear in the final creation.

⑨ Click Next Step.

Did You Know?

You can preselect your calendar images in Organizer before you begin the creation process. In the Photo Browser, Ctrl+click the images you want to use, and then click Create in the menu bar. When you come to the Arrange Your Photos window in the creation process, Organizer automatically imports your selected images.

Caution!

Organizer uses one photo for each month as well as for the title page. When you expand calendar dates, you also need images for each additional month. For example, if you select 25 images for a 36-month calendar, then Organizer prompts you to import additional images, or to approve the use of blank pages for the months without a corresponding image.

Create a
PHOTO WALL CALENDAR

When you create a photo wall calendar with Organizer, you can rearrange the order of the calendar images after you import them. Organizer labels each image with the month to which you assign it in the calendar. When you click and drag the images around to rearrange them, Organizer automatically relabels them according to their new placement.

You can also scale the images. When you click an image on the calendar page, a bounding box appears around the image. You can then click and drag the

bounding box to scale the image in any direction. When you are finished, the image frame displays only that part of the resized image that is within the frame area.

You can also move the image within the frame by clicking and dragging it to anywhere within the bounding box. This enables you to reposition a scaled image to change the subject focus within the frame area. You can reposition and rescale the image by clicking the image and moving or scaling it again.

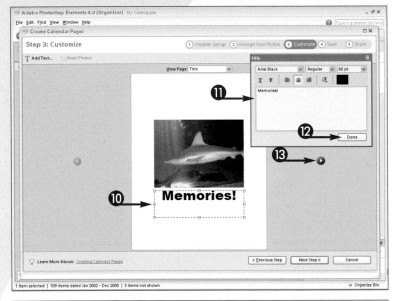

The Customize window appears.

⑩ Double-click the text box.

⑪ Type and format your text in the window that appears.

⑫ Click Done.

⑬ Click here to advance to the next month.

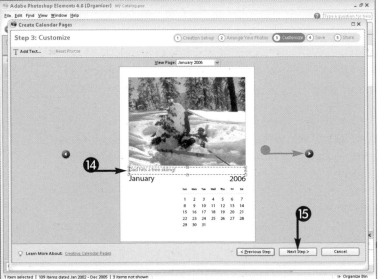

The inside calendar page template appears.

⑭ Double-click the text box to edit the caption.

● You can click here to advance to the next month.

⑮ When you have finished editing the captions, click Next Step.

The Save window appears.

⑯ Type a name for the calendar creation.

● Click this check box to use the calendar title as the filename (☐ changes to ☑).

⑰ Click Save.

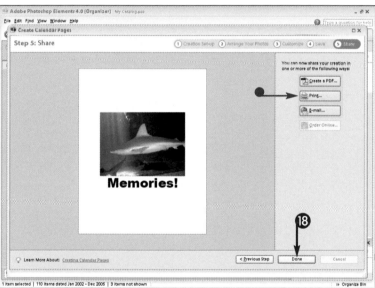

The Share window appears.

● You can select one of several ways in which to share the calendar.

⑱ Click Done.

TIPS

Caution!
Remember that when you increase the scale of an image, you are also enlarging all of the pixels within the image, which can result in a grainy photo. You should preview the image as a full page by clicking the Full Screen Preview button located in the upper-right corner of the step screen. This allows you to accurately preview the final image. You should always use high-resolution images to prevent pixelation of your scaled images.

Customize It!
You can use collections to quickly create a calendar in Organizer. In the Collections palette, select the collection you want by clicking the check box next to the collection name (☐ changes to ☑), and then click the Create button. Organizer automatically imports the images in your collection into the Calendar creation.

Exploring the Features in Photoshop Organizer

Photoshop Organizer is a great way to sort, tag, and design your personal photos. Organizer has features to help you store, protect, and share your images. You can also affect different aspects of Organizer, like basic file options, tag sorting orders, or settings for hardware such as scanners, digital cameras, and more through the Preferences command dialog box.

You can spend innumerable hours taking photos, importing them into your catalog, and designing creations using the images. The Archive or Backup features can protect your catalog file from damage or loss by saving them to a hard drive, portable memory card, or compact disc. You must have the available hardware necessary to utilize these features.

Organizer has several ways to view your images. The Calendar feature enables you to sort and review your images based on actual calendar timelines and by marking special events. Photo Review allows you to view images in a full-screen photo slide show while Photo Compare brings photos next to each other so you can compare small details, a very useful function for photo selection.

You can share your images by e-mail directly through Organizer and your default e-mail program. Organizer gives you some very creative ways to share your photographs with family or friends. There is also a feature that enables you to create and save contact information for people or groups that you share with regularly.

Top 100

Share creations using
E-MAIL

Along with making it easier to organize and work with your images, Photoshop Organizer also allows you to easily share them through e-mail. You can select any image and quickly e-mail it to a friend or family member through the Internet. All that you need is an Internet connection and a default e-mail program. Windows uses Outlook Express as its default e-mail program, as shown in this example.

To share a creation, you can simply click an image, and then tell Organizer that you want to send it as

an image attachment. Organizer then allows you to type in the e-mail address of your intended recipient, write a message, and even define how Organizer attaches the image to the e-mail.

You can also send multiple images by first selecting them, and then selecting the e-mail feature. This is a great way to share many of your favorite pictures quickly and easily. If you want, you can also add images during the e-mail process.

① Click the photo you want to send by e-mail.

② Click File.

③ Click E-mail.

If a dialog box appears asking you to select a client, select your e-mail program and click Continue.

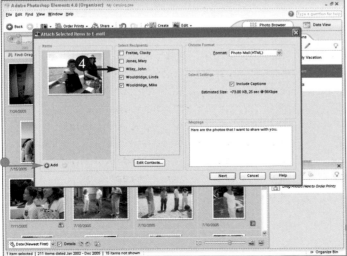

The Attach Selected Items to E-mail dialog box appears.

● You can click here to add or remove images.

④ Click the check boxes next to the recipients to whom you want to send the photo (☐ changes to ☑).

Note: For information about adding new recipients, see Task #93.

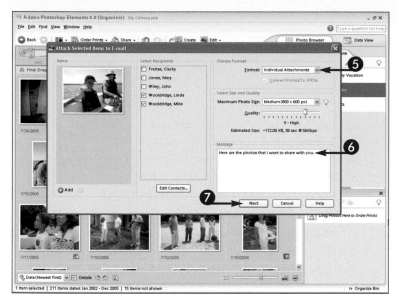

5 Click here and select an e-mail format.

Note: *For more information about using Stationery, see Task #92.*

6 Type your e-mail message.

7 Click Next.

DIFFICULTY LEVEL

Organizer opens your default e-mail application with your message ready to send.

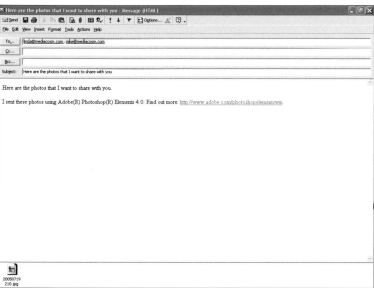

TIPS

Did You Know?

You can quickly e-mail multiple photos by using Tags, Favorites, or Collections. Simply click the check box next to the group you want in the palette (□ changes to ☑), then click File, and then click Attach to E-mail. You can also e-mail individual images from these groups, thus taking advantage of Organizer's quick sorting abilities.

Customize It!

Many e-mail servers use anti-virus software that blocks certain common file types, including graphic formats such as JPG, GIF, and BMP. If your recipient is using this software, then you can use the Simple Slide Show (PDF) format selection. The PDF format is widely accepted for business documents and is usually accepted by e-mail servers.

Embed e-mail images using
STATIONERY

Although many people send images as e-mail attachments, Organizer now allows you to add graphic design elements to your e-mail using Stationery. When you select a background design and frame for your image or images, Stationery sends them as attractive graphics within your e-mail message. It does this by generating the HTML code that places the image and accompanying design elements directly into your e-mail message.

Organizer offers a selection of 52 different stationeries, and then customizes the layout design

based on the stationery that you choose. You can also choose from different backgrounds, fonts, image layouts, colors, and borders to create a unique design for your photographs. You can also type a message that appears on your stationery, and apply different fonts and font styles to the message.

You can choose from eight different layouts that allow you to display multiple images in the stationery of your choice. You can use five different image-size options that enable you to further customize the appearance of your e-mail.

① Click File.

② Click E-mail.

The Attach Selected Items to E-mail dialog box appears.

③ Click to select the recipients (☐ changes to ☑).

Note: For more information about e-mail options, see Task #91.

④ Select Photo Mail (HTML) in the Format menu.

⑤ Click Next.

The Stationery & Layouts Wizard screen appears.

⑥ Click the stationery type you want.

● A full-size sample appears.

⑦ Click Next Step.

The Customize the Layout screen appears.

⑧ Select the background, layout, text, and border options that you want.

⑨ Click Next.

92

DIFFICULTY LEVEL

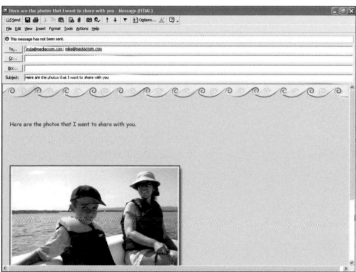

Organizer opens your default e-mail application with your custom photo-mail message ready to send.

TIPS

Caution!

Keep in mind that each image that you add increases the total file size. You should limit the number and quality of your images to prevent this from happening. Many e-mail servers impose file-size limits that block large files, or allow limited storage space, which can also result in your e-mail being rejected. You can send your images in PDF format to reduce your file size.

Did You Know?

The stationery styles in the Stationery & Layouts Wizard can include captions that appear next to your photos. You can click the caption text in the Wizard to edit them. The text options that you select in the Customize the Layout window apply to the captions. You can turn off captions by deselecting the Include Captions option in the Attach Selected Items to E-mail dialog box.

Create a
CONTACT BOOK

You can store important information about family, friends, and colleagues using the Contact Book feature in Organizer. You can create a collection of e-mail addresses and cell phone numbers for each person to whom you want to send your images. This enables you to quickly select your recipient from a list when you send an e-mail.

The Contact Book feature also allows you to store other personal information, such as mailing addresses and phone numbers, for your contacts. This contact information is then readily available when you need it.

You can also create contact groups in Organizer, in which you place numerous contacts under a single descriptive name. This is a very useful feature when you have regular groups of individuals with whom you share photographs. This feature enables you to select the entire group with a single mouse click when you create an e-mail message. You can easily add and remove contacts, making it easy to keep these groups up to date.

① Click Edit.

② Click Contact Book.

The Contact Book dialog box opens.

③ Click New Contact.

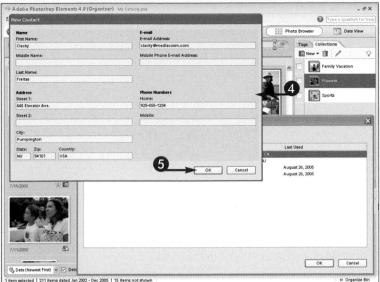

The New Contact dialog box appears.

93
DIFFICULTY LEVEL

④ Type the name, address, and other information.

⑤ Click OK.

● The new contact appears in the Contact Book.

Note: To send a photo to a contact by e-mail, see Task #91.

⑥ Click OK to close the Contact Book.

TIPS

Customize It!

To quickly create an e-mail contact group, simply click the New Group button in the Contact Book dialog box. When the New Group dialog box appears, type a name for your new group. You can then select existing contacts and add them to your new group. Your group now appears in the Contact Book. You can quickly add or remove contacts for this group by clicking the group icon and then clicking Edit.

Did You Know?

You can delete multiple contacts from the Contact Book. Ctrl+click the contacts that you want to remove and then click Delete. Organizer asks you to confirm the deletions. If you click OK, then Organizer deletes all of the contacts that you selected.

View files with
DATE VIEW

Organizer enables you to view and sort image files in many ways. For example, Calendar view organizes your images by date and displays them in a calendar format. Organizer draws attention to dates that contain images.

You can view your images by the year, month, or day. Each view generates a different calendar, and allows you to enter notes for particular dates. These notes do not appear in the image metadata, but are assigned to the date instead.

In Year view, the calendar shows dates for the entire year, with dates that contain images or common holidays appearing in a different color. Month view displays a one-month calendar, with a thumbnail appearing in the squares of any dates that contain images. The thumbnail is the first image taken for that day. Daily view shows a large version of the first image for that day. Each view allows you to review all images for a particular day or to create an event that is associated with that day.

① Click Date View.

Organizer switches to Date View.

② Click a date.

● You can hold the cursor over the date to view the image count and event information for that date.

● You can type information about this date in the Daily Note field.

③ Click the Month button.

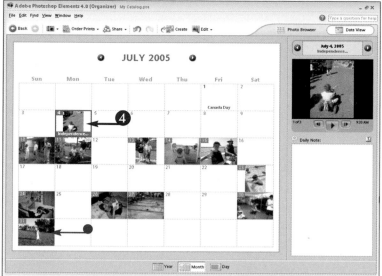

Organizer switches
to the Month view.

● Image thumbnails
appear on each date
that contains photos.

❹ Double-click a day.

Organizer switches to the Day view for
that day.

● You can click the thumbnails to view the
different photos from that day.

● You can click the Play button to play a
slide show.

❺ Click Photo Browser to switch back to the
default Organizer view.

TIPS

Customize It!

You can customize your Date view layout
and information. Click Edit, then click
Preferences, and then click Calendar.
You can add or remove specific dates
from a list of common holidays, or
you can add your own event date to
Date view. This feature is useful when
you want to quickly edit Date view, or
to restore the Organizer defaults.

Did You Know?

You can quickly navigate through dates.
You can click the arrows on either side
of the date that appears at the top of
the calendar, or you can click the arrows
in the Preview box. Depending on the
view, you can also click the date at the
top of the calendar to select a particular
year or month.

Add an
EVENT in Date view

You can use Date view to create special markers in your calendar. A marker acts as a place card for an actual date or occasion. You can use a marker, known as an event, to highlight special occasions that do not appear on the holiday list, but that are important to you, such as anniversaries, birthdays, and vacations.

You can make any date on the calendar into an event, even a date that has another event attached to it, such as a national holiday. You can specify a

name for the event, the date, and how often it happens. You can then add photos that pertain to your event. You can also add or delete as many events as you like.

You should not confuse events with event tags or other organizing tools. Although you can assign event tags to individual images in order to help you to sort and find specific pictures, events are simply identifying names that you associate with a particular date.

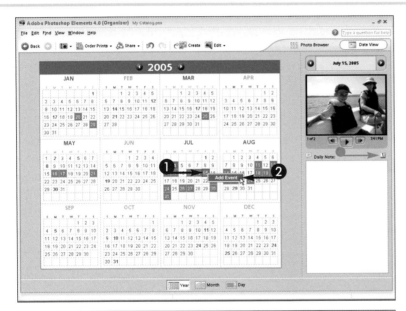

① In Date View, right-click the date of an event.

② Click Add Event.

● You can also click the New Event button above the Daily Note area.

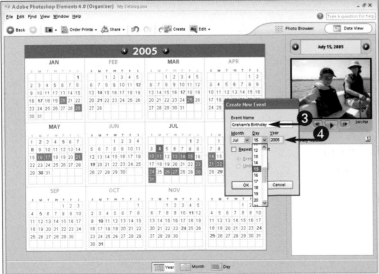

The Create New Event dialog box appears.

③ Type a name for your event.

④ Click here to select the date or dates of the event.

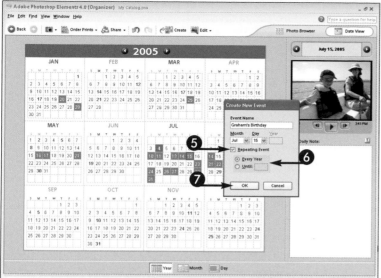

⑤ Click the check box next to Repeating Event if it is an annual event (☐ changes to ☑).

⑥ Click a radio button to specify how often the event occurs (○ changes to ⊙).

⑦ Click OK.

Organizer applies your changes.

⑧ Right-click the new event date on your calendar.

⑨ Click Delete Event.

The new event appears in the pop-up list.

⑩ Click an event in the pop-up list to remove it from this date.

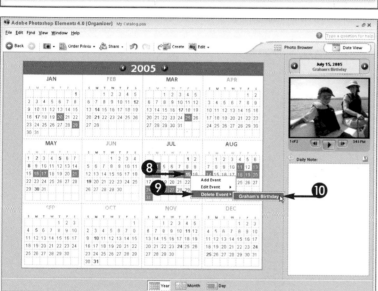

TIPS

Customize It!

You can right-click any date to add to or delete events that you have specified for that date. While you cannot delete a permanent date such as a national holiday, you can turn it on and off in the Preferences menu. Simply click Edit, then click Preferences, and then click Calendar. You can then specify which holidays you want to appear in Date view.

Caution!

Because digital camera dates are sometimes incorrect, your images may appear in the wrong date on your calendar. You can reset the date of an image in either Date view or the Photo Browser. Right-click any image in the Photo Browser, or right-click the image in the daily preview and select Adjust Date and Time from the pop-up list.

View your images in
FULL SCREEN VIEW

Organizer offers a Full Screen View feature that allows you to view a group of images in a large slide show format. You can use the feature to decide which images you want to keep or remove from a collection, correct minor photo adjustments to color or contrast, or even rotate a photograph. Full Screen view allows you to easily assign Tags and Categories to your images using pop-up menus.

In Full Screen view, you can watch the slide show manually clicking from one image to the next, or you

can run it automatically. The automatic slide show rotates through your selected images and displays them based on your preferences. For example, you can include captions and specify the length of time that each image remains on-screen.

You can also add background music to an automatic slide show in one of three audio formats, MP3, WAV, or WMA. You can use any audio file from your computer in the slide show as long as it is in one of these formats.

① Ctrl+click to select the images you want to appear in your slide show.

② Click View.

③ Click View Photos in Full Screen.

The Full Screen View Options dialog box appears.

④ Click here and select the background music you want.

⑤ Click here to specify how long you want each image to appear on-screen.

⑥ Click these check boxes to specify other options (☐ changes to ☑).

⑦ Click OK.

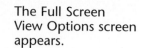

The Full Screen View Options screen appears.

⑧ Click here to rotate the current image.

⑨ Click here to access a drop-down menu of additional features.

⑩ Click here to adjust the zoom on your image.

⑪ Click the Play button.

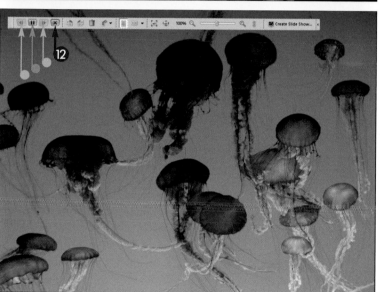

Organizer plays the slide show.

● You can click the Pause button to pause the slide show.

● You can click the Forward and Back buttons to move between slides.

⑫ When you are finished, click the Exit button.

TIPS

Did You Know?
You can also play audio captions in your slide show. You can record audio narration for an image as part of its base information. When you select this option, Photo Review plays any audio captions along with the background music.

Customize It!
You can use the Zoom slider in the toolbar to quickly zoom in to check image detail, or zoom out to view the entire picture. You can also click the Fit on Screen button or the Actual Pixels button to automatically adjust the images to fit your screen.

Using
PHOTO COMPARE
to select an image

When you need to decide between similar images in a project, you can use the Photo Compare feature in Organizer to quickly determine which image you want to use. With Photo Compare, you can view two images next to each other to focus in on and to compare the details of each image. You can view the images side by side, or above and below each other.

Photo Compare enables you to use the Zoom feature to view very minute sections of an image that would

be difficult to view at a normal size. The Zoom feature allows you to quickly change the view of your image by either clicking the Zoom In or Zoom Out buttons or by dragging the slider. You can also use the Synch Pan and Zoom feature to coordinate movement between both images simultaneously, so that you can compare image details in the same locations without switching and adjusting each image separately.

① Ctrl+click the images you want to compare.

② Click View.

③ Click Compare Photos Side by Side.

The Compare Photos Side by Side screen appears.

④ Click the Sync Pan and Zoom button.

⑤ Click and drag the Zoom slider.

The two images zoom simultaneously to the same relative location.

6 Click the Layout drop-down arrow.

7 Click Above and Below.

Organizer changes to Above and Below view.

● You can click here to select the Fit on Screen or Actual Pixels zoom option.

8 When you are finished, click the Exit button.

TIPS

Customize It!

You can also use Photo Compare to edit and assign your images. In the toolbar, click the Action Menu button. The drop-down menu displays functions such as Smart Fix, and allows you to assign tags and categories, as well as show image properties. You can select and mark the images you want without returning to the Photo Browser.

Did You Know?

You can also use the Photo Review feature while in Photo Compare. The two features share toolbars and areas, and you can switch back and forth between them by clicking the Photo Review button or the Photo Compare button in the toolbar. For more information about Photo Review, see Task #96.

ARCHIVE
your photos to CD-ROM

You can use the Archive feature in Organizer to preserve, share, and store your images. Image collections can take up a lot of space on a hard drive, and this can slow your system performance as well as image processing in programs such as Organizer. Your system or hard drive may also fail, causing irreplaceable data loss.

You can use the Archive feature to save your full-resolution, original images to a CD-ROM as an archive. You can also use the Archive feature to create CD-ROMs for sending images to print or for sharing images with friends, family, and colleagues.

The Archive feature enables you to save your files in one of two ways. Either you can copy your images to CD-ROM, or you can move them to CD-ROM while simultaneously removing the images from your hard drive. Copying is a good way to back up your images while still having them available on your computer. Moving your images to CD-ROM enables you to free up hard drive space and to save your images to a permanent media.

① Click File.

② Click Burn.

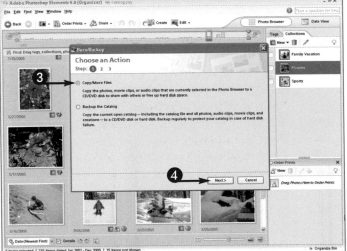

The Burn/Backup dialog box appears.

③ Click Copy/Move Files (○ changes to ●).

④ Click Next.

The Copy/Move Options screen appears.

● If you want to delete images from your hard drive after copying them, click Move Files (☐ changes to ☑).

This example leaves the check box unchecked and does not delete the files after copying.

⑤ Click Next.

The Destination Settings screen appears.

⑥ Click the CD-burning drive you want to use.

⑦ Type a name for your CD-ROM.

⑧ Click here to select the write speed.

⑨ Click Done.

Organizer writes to the CD-ROM.

TIPS

Caution!
When you archive your files, you should create a copy of your archived CD-ROM, in case the original CD-ROM is accidentally damaged. Organizer allows you to create an archive with copy only, and then to copy the archive using the Move method. This technique allows you to make multiple copies and to free up space on your computer.

Did You Know?
Archiving your images with the Move option will not delete them from your catalog. As a catalog reference, low-resolution copies of your images are created. If you want to use one of these moved images, you will receive a prompt asking you to insert the archive disc containing the original image.

BACK UP PHOTOS
on your computer

You can use Organizer to protect against file loss on your computer by using its Backup function. Backup burns a recoverable copy of your entire catalog, including images, video clips, audio clips, tags, collections, and other Organizer features. This helps protect against accidental loss through hardware failure or theft of your computer.

When you back up your catalog, you save the images and tags, but also the folder structure and organization for use in Windows. You can use the backup function to save to an internal or external hard drive or to any portable media such as CD-R or DVD+/-R discs.

You have two kinds of backup — Full Backup and Incremental Backup. Full backup is recommended for the first backup session or for saving after any major changes to your catalog. Full backup will completely compile all original and edited files to save. Incremental Backup utilizes the original backup as a base, and only updates or saves images imported or edited since the last backup. This is useful for keeping up to date with frequent changes to your catalog.

① Click File.

② Click Backup.

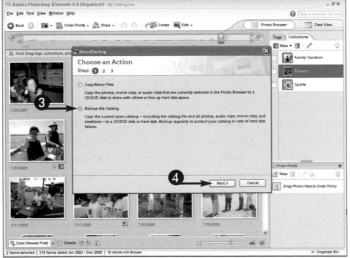

The Burn/Backup dialog box appears.

③ Click Backup the Catalog
(○ changes to ⊙).

④ Click Next.

A Missing Files dialog box may appear. You can click Reconnect to search for missing files before backing up.

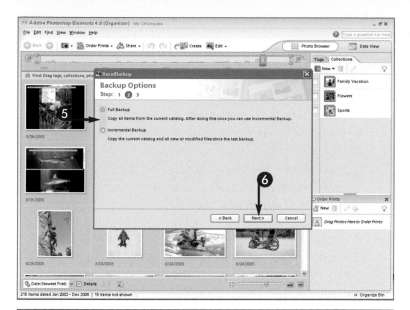

The Backup Options screen appears.

5 Click the backup type you want (○ changes to ◉).

Note: If this is your first backup, you should choose Full Backup.

6 Click Next.

DIFFICULTY LEVEL

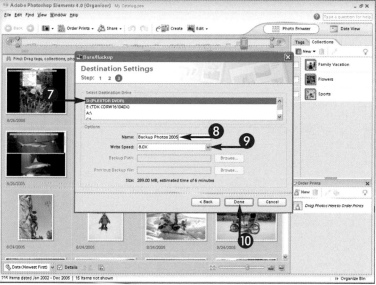

The Destination Settings screen appears.

7 Click the CD-burning drive you want to use.

8 Type a name for your backup CD-ROM.

9 Click here to select the write speed.

10 Click Done.

Organizer writes to your backup CD-ROM.

 TIPS

Customize It!

If you regularly use many images, then you should set up a regular schedule for backing up your catalogs. This helps you to ensure that recent edits or additions are not lost in a system failure. If you are a professional user, then it is vital that you schedule regular backups.

Customize It!

When you use the Backup function with multiple discs, each disc is labeled sequentially with reference information. When you use the Incremental Backup and create additional discs, Organizer requests the last disc in the latest backup and updates the catalog and disc information to include the new discs sequentially in the original set.

Set your organizer
PREFERENCES

Organizer offers many functions and features, and each has its own set of options. You can specify some options while you are using a feature, while other settings are available in the Preferences dialog box. These settings affect how these features behave and appear in Organizer, and include Display, E-mail, Calendar, and Tags and Collections.

When you access the Preferences dialog box, Organizer displays 10 different areas that you can adjust. For example, you can tell Organizer how to import images from a scanner or digital camera, or

to update your Adobe Elements and Organizer software automatically.

Each Preferences dialog box also contains a Restore Default Settings button, which resets all preferences to their default values. You can use this feature when the settings cause Organizer to behave in an unexpected or unusual way. For example, when you reference a supplementary editing application in the Editing preferences, the program may not be installed on your computer, or a referenced file may have been deleted.

① Click Edit.

② Click Preferences.

③ Click General.

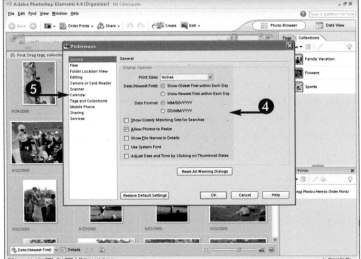

The Preferences dialog box appears.

④ Specify the preferences you want for your general display options.

⑤ Click Calendar.

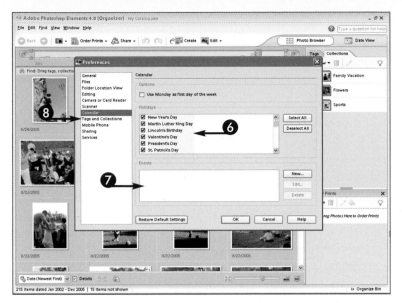

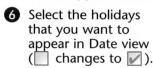

The Calendar screen appears.

⑥ Select the holidays that you want to appear in Date view (☐ changes to ☑).

⑦ Edit the events you have created for Date view.

⑧ Click Tags and Collections.

DIFFICULTY LEVEL

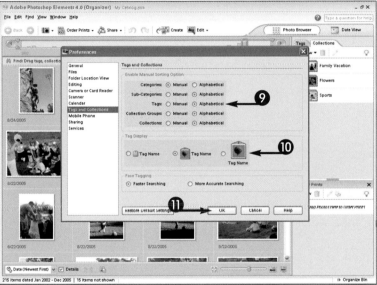

The Tags and Collections screen appears.

⑨ Click here to specify your sorting options.

⑩ Click here to specify a tag display size.

⑪ Click OK.

Organizer closes the Preferences dialog box.

Did You Know?
You can access preferences for Elements from within Organizer. Click Edit, then click Preferences, and then click Editor Preferences. Organizer switches over to Elements, and opens the Elements Preferences dialog box. You can return to the Organizer preferences by clicking Organize and Share in the Elements Preferences drop-down menu.

Caution!
You may have many different preference settings in Organizer. When you use the Restore Default Settings button, Organizer resets all preferences, not just those on-screen. You should be careful not to undo a preference that you want to keep.

Index

Index

Index

Index

Index

5/06

Want more simplified tips and tricks?

Take a look at these

All designed for visual learners—just like you!

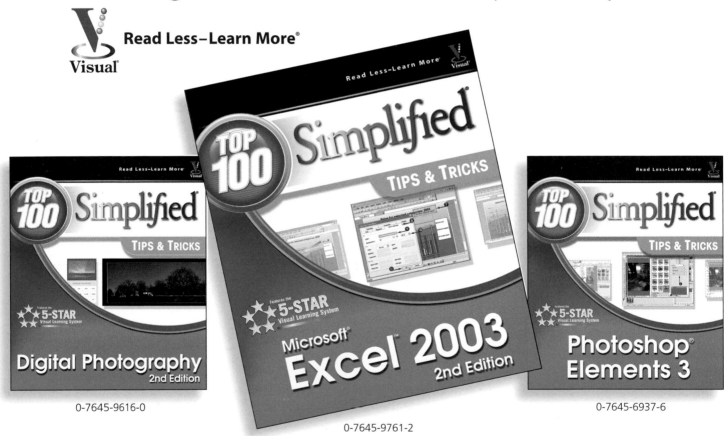

Read Less–Learn More®

Visual®

TOP 100 Simplified TIPS & TRICKS
Digital Photography 2nd Edition
0-7645-9616-0

TOP 100 Simplified TIPS & TRICKS
Microsoft® Excel™ 2003 2nd Edition
0-7645-9761-2

TOP 100 Simplified TIPS & TRICKS
Photoshop® Elements 3
0-7645-6937-6

For a complete listing of *Top 100 Simplified*® *Tips & Tricks* titles and other Visual books, go to wiley.com/go/visualtech

Wiley, the Wiley logo, the Visual logo, Read Less-Learn More, and Simplified are trademarks or registered trademarks of John Wiley & Sons, Inc. and/or its affiliates. All other trademarks are the property of their respective owners.

Visual®
An Imprint of ⊕WILEY
Now you know.